DATE DUE

DEMCO 38-296

Women of the 1960s

Titles in the Women in History series include:

WOMEN
IN
HISTORY

Women of
the 1960s

Stuart A. Kallen

LUCENT
BOOKS®

THOMSON
———— ✦ ————
GALE

San Diego • Detroit • New York • San Francisco • Cleveland • New Haven, Conn. • Waterville, Maine • London • Munich

Cover Image: A photograph of demonstrators at the 1968 Miss America Pageant.

© 2003 by Lucent Books. Lucent Books is an imprint of The Gale Group, Inc.,
a division of Thomson Learning, Inc.

Lucent Books® and Thomson Learning™ are trademarks used herein under license.

For more information, contact
Lucent Books
27500 Drake Rd.
Farmington Hills, MI 48331-3535
Or you can visit our Internet site at http://www.gale.com

LIBRARY OF CONGRESS CATALOGING-IN-PUBLICATION DATA

Kallen, Stuart A., 1955–
   Women of the 1960s / by Stuart A. Kallen.
     p. cm. — (Women in history series)
Includes bibliographical references (p.) and index.
   ISBN 1-59018-251-0 (alk. paper)
  1. Women—United States—History—20th century—Juvenile literature. 2.
Women's rights—United States—History—20th century—Juvenile literature. 3.
Women—United States—Social conditions—Juvenile literature. I. Title. II. Series.
   HQ1421 .K245 2003
   305.42'0973—dc21

                  2002015474

Printed in the United States of America

Contents

Foreword

The story of the past as told in traditional historical writings all too often leaves the impression that if men are not the only actors in the narrative, they are assuredly the main characters. With a few notable exceptions, males were the political, military, and economic leaders in virtually every culture throughout recorded time. Since traditional historical scholarship focuses on the public arenas of government, foreign relations, and commerce, the actions and ideas of men—or at least of powerful men—are naturally at the center of conventional accounts of the past.

In the last several decades, however, many historians have abandoned their predecessors' emphasis on "great men" to explore the past "from the bottom up," a phenomenon that has had important consequences for the study of women's history. These social historians, as they are known, focus on the day-to-day experiences of the "silent majority"—those people typically omitted from conventional scholarship because they held relatively little political or economic sway within their societies. In the new social history, members of ethnic and racial minorities, factory workers, peasants, slaves, children,

and women are no longer relegated to the background but are placed at the very heart of the narrative.

Around the same time social historians began broadening their research to include women and other previously neglected elements of society, the feminist movement of the late 1960s and 1970s was also bringing unprecedented attention to the female heritage. Feminists hoped that by examining women's past experiences, contemporary women could better understand why and how gender-based expectations had developed in their societies, as well as how they might reshape inherited—and typically restrictive—economic, social, and political roles in the future.

Today, some four decades after the feminist and social history movements gave new impetus to the study of women's history, there is a rich and continually growing body of work on all aspects of women's lives in the past. The Lucent Books Women in History series draws upon this abundant and diverse literature to introduce students to women's experiences within a variety of past cultures and time periods in terms of the distinct roles they filled. In their capacities as workers, activists, and artists, women exerted significant influence on important events whether they conformed to or broke from traditional roles. The Women in History titles depict extraordinary women who managed to attain positions of influence in their male-dominated societies, including such celebrated heroines as the feisty medieval queen Eleanor of Aquitaine, the brilliant propagandist of the American Revolution Mercy Otis Warren, and the courageous African American activist of the Civil War era Harriet Tubman. Included as well are the stories of the ordinary—and often overlooked—women of the past who also helped shape their societies myriad ways—moral, intellectual, and economic—without straying far from customary gender roles: the housewives and mothers, school teachers and church volunteers, midwives and nurses and wartime camp followers.

In this series, readers will discover that many of these unsung women took more significant parts in the great political and social upheavals of their day than has often been recognized. In *Women of the American Revolution,* for example, students will learn how American housewives assumed a crucial role in helping the Patriots win the war against Britain. They accomplished this by planting and harvesting fields, producing and trading goods, and doing whatever else was necessary to maintain the family farm or business in the absence of their soldier husbands despite the heavy burden of housekeeping and child-care duties they already bore. By their self-sacrificing actions, competence, and ingenuity, these anonymous heroines not only kept their families alive, but kept the economy of their struggling young nation going as well during eight long years of war.

Each volume in this series contains generous commentary from the works of respected contemporary scholars, but the Women in History series particularly emphasizes quotations from primary sources such as diaries, letters, and journals whenever possible to allow the women of the past to speak for themselves. These firsthand accounts not only help students to better understand the dimensions of women's daily spheres—the work they did, the organizations they belonged to, the physical hardships they faced—but also how they viewed themselves and their actions in the light of their society's expectations for their sex.

The distinguished American historian Mary Beard once wrote that women have always been a "force in history." It is hoped that the books in this series will help students to better appreciate the vital yet often little-known ways in which women of the past have shaped their societies and cultures.

Introduction:
A Decade of Profound Social Change

The 1960s were a time of drastic change and ferocious turmoil in the United States, when Americans of every generation, but particularly the young, seriously questioned nearly all basic, long-held cultural beliefs. The decade was marked by disillusionment after the assassinations of charismatic and progressive leaders such as John F. Kennedy, his brother and presidential candidate Robert Kennedy, and civil rights pioneer Martin Luther King Jr. It was a decade of war and protest as more than 1 million Americans were called to fight in Vietnam while an equal number took to the streets in sometimes violent protests against the war. And as the war raged in Vietnam, the streets of inner-city America also began to look like war zones as major riots broke out year after year in largely African American urban neighborhoods. Meanwhile, the consumption of LSD—a powerful and relatively new drug—by millions of Americans spawned a counterculture generation of hippies whose guiding philosophies revolved around peace, love, sexual freedom, and rock and roll.

Although no one looking at the world in 1960 could have imagined the incredible societal transformations that would take place by 1970, a few social scientists might have seen the changes coming. The battles over war, peace, love, sex, religion, politics, and drugs were largely an outgrowth of the baby boom generation coming of age.

Baby Boomer Women Come of Age

In 1945, at the end of World War II, the population of the United States was less than half of what it is today—around 141 million. But between 1946 and 1964 more than 75 million American women and men were born—more than 4 million a year during the mid-1950s. (At the boom's peak in 1957, a baby was born every seven seconds in America.) This baby boom represented a huge demographic "bubble" that moved through society for decades overshadowing both the previous generation and the generations that followed.

Over half of the baby boomers were girls, and by 1960 women constituted a majority in America, making up 53 percent of the total population. Sheer numbers notwithstanding, throughout much of the decade women were generally shut out of most jobs customarily performed by men. Women, if they worked outside the home at all, disproportionally filled traditional roles such as teaching, nursing, office work, cooking, housekeeping, and so on. This description applied well outside the mainstream: Even during the heyday of the revolutionary antiwar and countercultural struggles, women within those movements were by and large expected to fill a variety of domestic or supporting roles.

The Pill

Despite these traditional limitations, female baby boomers coming of age during the sixties were faced with entirely different circumstances than those experienced by their mothers. The most revolutionary development for women was the introduction of the birth-control pill in 1960.

The advent of the birth-control pill in 1960 allowed women to choose when to start their families.

In 1950 the Planned Parenthood Foundation of America donated $2,100 to American biologist Gregory Pincus to develop an ideal contraceptive—stipulating that it be simple and practical, reliable, harmless, and acceptable to both husbands and wives. With additional government and private funding, research produced the first commercial oral contraceptive in 1960. Enovid-10, or, as it quickly became known universally, "the Pill," was 99 percent effective—more effective than any other means of birth control except surgical sterilization. By the end of the decade, millions of American women were preventing pregnancy by swallowing a pill, and the life of women and of the family was rewritten.

With an inexpensive, relatively safe, and convenient method of preventing pregnancy, in an age before AIDS and before the legalization of abortion, "the Pill" ushered in a so-called sexual revolution without precedent. Although a majority of sixties women who used the pill were married, the oral contraceptive gave all women—single or married, rich or poor—options for roles beyond motherhood. Women were able to work, attend college, or pursue their dreams, starting families only when they were ready.

Higher Education

Female baby boomers in the 1960s were also the best-educated women in history.

Whereas only about 5 percent of women in the World War II generation went to college, up to 35 percent of female baby boomers attended institutions of higher learning. However, in a parallel to women's roles in the workforce, more than 75 percent of women pursued only six fields: English, fine arts, history, home economics, nursing, and teaching. And women who did study male-dominated subjects such as engineering or biology often wound up as teachers of these subjects rather than professional engineers or biologists.

One of the most striking effects of greater numbers of women on campus was the institution of the first women's studies programs in college curricula. During the 1960s the traditional curricula came under increasing scrutiny for bias in favor of the historical contributions and achievements of men, mostly elite white men. There was little focus on the experiences of women. Gradually academic institutions across the country addressed this imbalance with coursework and degree programs on women's historical and social contributions and gender-related issues. These programs prompted further scholarship by and about women and fueled the feminist movement of this and later decades.

Although job opportunities remained limited, the effects of an educated female populace were seen throughout the nation. On campus, women were exposed to new political ideas; the civil rights and the antiwar movements had their deepest roots in academia. Taking a cue from the civil rights movement, women began to question the gender discrimination and lack of equal rights for women in all levels of society and culture. And they acted together to generate widespread improvements in their lives throughout the following decades.

Positive and Permanent Change

In *American Women in the 1960s: Changing the Future,* Blanche Linden-Ward and Carol Hurd Green describe how these positive developments emerged during a time of violent protests, riots, and assassination:

> The sixties was a time of turbulence and social upheaval, but also one of promise and exhilaration. Amid civil disturbance and an escalating, seemingly endless war, people came together to create new communities and alliances and to say no to old prejudices [and] to acceptance of women's inferior status. . . . [The] sixties was a time of argument and ideas, with conversations seeking and including groups hitherto [ignored]. [1]

Today, few question whether a woman can perform a job equal to—or better than—a man. It is a commonly accepted notion that women can be world-class doctors, lawyers, politicians, business

Burning a draft card, a hippie woman protests the war in Vietnam.

executives, astronauts, and tennis players, if they so choose. Though controversy continues to rage over such gender issues as birth control, abortion, sexual harassment, and discrimination in the workplace, the legacy of the 1960s is apparent in the twenty-first century. Although antiwar, black power, and counterculture movements have faded into the backdrop of the modern world, changes enacted by women are now a seamless part of the social fabric. The injustice and sexual discrimination faced by today's mothers, grandmothers, and great-grandmothers is a now permanent part of history. And it was the women of the sixties who fought for an end to sexism and gender discrimination and set the stage for the rights enjoyed by today's American woman.

Chapter 1:
Women in the
Mainstream

❦

The 1960s are often remembered for their sweeping cultural changes and political unrest. But for a large majority of middle-class American women, the decade was a time of prosperity and calm. Throughout the 1960s, almost two out of three American women were housewives, cooking, cleaning, and rearing children at home while their husbands worked. This was at a time when the average married couple was able to own a home in the suburbs, buy a new car every few years, and send their children to college with the wages earned by a single family member.

The new American affluence—unavailable to most people before World War II—meant that women could marry and start families at a younger age. And in the early sixties, women married in larger numbers than ever before. In 1940 only 42 percent of women were married by the age of twenty-four, but by 1960 that number had jumped to 70 percent. And during the 1960s, the average age for marriage was lower than ever before—or since. The average age for women to marry during the mid-1960s was nineteen, for men twenty-two. In addition, 14 million girls were engaged by the age of seventeen, and more than 40 percent of all new brides were teenagers.

A Record Number of Young Mothers

Those who married and had children could seek out advice from a host of scholars and the media in glossy magazines such as *McCall's, Ladies' Home Journal, Life,* and *Redbook.* In *The Feminine Mystique,* Betty Friedan describes the situation:

> [Millions] of words [were] written about women, for women, in . . . books and articles by experts telling women their role was to seek fulfillment as wives and mothers. . . . Experts told them how to catch a man and keep him, how to breastfeed children and handle their toilet training, how to cope with sibling rivalry and adolescent rebellion; how to buy a dishwasher, bake bread, cook gourmet snails, and build a swimming

A young family gathers around the breakfast table in 1965. On average, women in the mid-1960s married by age nineteen.

pool with their own hands; how to dress, look, and act more feminine and make marriage more exciting; how to keep their husbands from dying young and their sons from growing into delinquents. They were taught to pity the neurotic, unfeminine, unhappy women who wanted to be poets or physicists or presidents. They learned that truly feminine women do not want careers, higher education, political rights—the independence and the opportunities that the old-fashioned feminists fought for [earlier in the century]. . . . A thousand expert voices applauded their femininity, their adjustment, their new maturity. All they had to do was devote their lives from earliest girlhood to finding a husband and bearing children. [2]

This widespread trend toward matrimony and childbearing resulted in an unprecedented population boom in the United States. Although the birth-control pill was introduced in 1960, it was not commonly used until the midsixties. In fact, in 1960 a record number of babies— 4.25 million—were born in the United States, compared to about half that many in 1940.

For many young mothers, the family unit had changed drastically since they themselves were children. Before World War II, due to housing shortages and tough economic times, married couples often raised their children in the same household with grandparents, brothers, sisters, aunts, uncles, and other extended family members. But in the sixties, "nuclear families" were made up of only a mother, father, and their children. These families went to church, went on vacation, saw ball games, worked in the yard, watched television, washed the car, and did nearly everything together. Without the helping hands of grandmothers, sisters, and aunts, however, suburban women had little help with household chores. As sociologist Helena Znaniecka Lopata writes in *Occupation: Housewife,* the sixties were "one of the few times in recorded history that the mother-child unit has been so isolated from adult assistance. Responsibilities for health, welfare, the behavior . . . of the child is basically unshared. The father is not held accountable for what happens to the children because he is not home most of the time." [3]

With women raising the children nearly single-handedly while men worked outside the home every day, sixties couples inhabited two separate environments. As Sonia Pressman Fuentes writes in the on-line article "Sex Maniac,"

> By and large, a woman's place was in the home. Her role was to marry and raise a family. If she was bright, common wisdom had it that she was to conceal her intelligence. She was to be attractive—but not too attractive. She was not to have career ambition, although she could work for a few years before marriage as a secretary, saleswoman, schoolteacher, telephone operator, or nurse. It was expected that she would be a virgin when she married. When she had children, she was to raise them differently so that they, too, would continue in the modes of behavior appropriate to their sex. If she divorced, which would reflect poorly on her, she might receive an award of alimony and child support— although it was unlikely that she would receive the monies for more than a few years. If she failed to marry, she was an old maid relegated to the periphery of life. . . .

> Women were not to be opinionated or assertive. They were expected to show an interest in fashion, books, ballet, cooking, sewing, knitting, and

volunteer activities. Political activities were acceptable as long as they were conducted behind the scenes. [4]

Women as Consumers

Although maintaining a nuclear family placed great pressures on the suburban housewife, she could depend on a wide array of modern appliances, such as washing machines and dryers, dishwashers, electric ranges, televisions, and stereo record players to make housework easier and more enjoyable. Supermarket shelves were filled with frozen foods, packaged meat, TV dinners, and other convenience foods that were unimaginable to a family during the 1930s or 1940s. And a profusion of new floor waxes, bathroom cleaners, laundry soaps, and other cleaning products competed for dollars in the household budget.

With industry producing so many new and improved products, American women took on a role as consumers, responsible for up to 75 percent of the nonbusiness purchases made in the United States in any given year. And with such buying power, women became the focus of the multibillion-dollar advertising industry.

Executives in the ad business surveyed tens of thousands of women and even hired psychologists to help shape the advertising messages. Since sixties women were better educated than previous generations, advertisers tailored their message to appeal to their creativity and desire for respect in order to sell their products. A study produced by an unnamed advertising agency selling cleaning products illustrates this point:

> One of the ways that the housewife raises her own prestige as cleaner of her home is through the use of specialized products for specialized tasks. . . .

> When she uses one product for washing clothes, a second for dishes, a third for walls, a fourth for floors, a fifth for venetian blinds, etc., rather than an all-purpose cleaner, she feels less like an unskilled laborer, more like an engineer, an expert.

> A second way of raising her own stature is to "do things my way"—to establish an expert's role for herself by creating her own "tricks of the trade." For example, she may "always put a bit of bleach in all my washing—even colored, to make them really clean!"

> Help her to justify her menial task by building up her role as the protector of her family—the killer of millions of microbes and germs. [5]

Hardworking Housewives

While advertisers analyzed women's roles as household "engineers," social scientists

A housewife displays a pan cleaned by Vel detergent. In the 1960s advertisers targeted women as consumers.

and pollsters studied their attitudes, hopes, and dreams. An extensive 1962 poll conducted by George Gallup for the *Saturday Evening Post* revealed that 96 percent of American housewives considered themselves satisfied with their lives as mothers and wives. Those interviewed for the poll were quoted as saying, "Few people are as happy as a housewife. . . . Being subordinate to men is part of being feminine. A women's prestige comes from her husband's opinion of her. Women who ask for equality fight nature."[6] Despite the statements and statistics, however, a full 90 percent also hoped that their daughters would not follow in their footsteps; rather, they hoped they would delay marriage and childbearing in order to attain a better education and find a useful career.

This curious inconsistency revealed that although most women seemed happy as housewives, they felt that the role had negative aspects as well. This was reflected in a study that showed that a typical suburban housewife put in an exhausting one-hundred-hour workweek caring for a husband, three children, a house, and a yard. (This compares to a forty-hour workweek for the husband.) This demanding schedule was detailed in a 1960 issue of *Parent's Magazine:*

> Every week the average American mother of three children washes 750 dishes and 400 pieces of silver; handles 250 articles of laundry; makes beds 35 times; shops for, carries, sorts, stores, and cooks 175 pounds of food; and walks 35 miles—just in her kitchen! . . . only a small part of what is expected of her.[7]

"Hopelessly Neurotic"

For some, this daily succession of cooking and cleaning proved to be lonely, isolating, and disheartening. In 1963 Betty Friedan released the groundbreaking book *The Feminine Mystique,* which revealed that although millions of women were told that they could only find happiness in the "feminine" roles of wife and mother, this "feminine mystique" did not provide true satisfaction. As Friedan writes,

> If a woman had a problem in the . . . 1960's, she knew that something must be wrong with her marriage, or with herself. Other women were sat-isfied with their lives, she thought. What kind of a woman was she if she did not feel this mysterious fulfill-ment waxing the kitchen floor? She was so ashamed to admit her dissat-isfaction that she never knew how many other women shared it. If she tried to tell her husband, he didn't understand what she was talking about. She did not really understand it herself. . . . [Women] in America found it harder to talk about this problem than about sex. . . . When a woman went to a psychiatrist for help, as many women did, she would say, "I'm so ashamed," or "I must be hopelessly neurotic." "I don't know what's wrong with women today," a suburban psychiatrist said uneasily. "I only know something is wrong because most of my patients happen to be women."[8]

Doctors who listened to these suburban women talk about anxiety and depression were quick to prescribe drugs such as barbiturates or tranquilizers to calm them down or amphetamine "pep pills" to help them speed through the day. By the midsixties, drugstores were filling over 100 million prescriptions a year for various sedatives, antidepressants, and other powerful mood-controlling drugs. When the tranquilizer Valium was invented in 1967, it quickly became the most popular legal drug in the United States. Although

The Feminine Mystique

Although national magazines and media avidly promoted marriage and children for women, some housewives were unhappy with their lives. When Betty Friedan, a suburban mother of three and a freelance writer, attended the fifteenth reunion of Smith College's class of 1942, she conducted a survey of her classmates and discovered that, in spite of their overall prosperous lives, many women were extremely unhappy because of their limited roles in society. In 1963 Friedan wrote about these findings in *The Feminine Mystique*, which became an instant best-seller. Calling this unhappiness "the problem that has no name," Friedan wrote,

The problem lay buried, unspoken, for many years in the minds of American women. It was a strange stirring, a sense of dissatisfaction, a yearning that women suffered in the middle of the twentieth century in the United States. Each suburban wife struggled with it alone. As she made the beds, shopped for groceries, matched slipcover material, ate peanut butter sandwiches with her children, chauffeured Cub Scouts and Brownies, lay beside her husband at night—she was afraid to ask even of herself the silent question—"Is this all [there is to life]?"

Friedan blamed women's magazines, television, advertising, and American popular culture for this widespread unhappiness. These institutions promised that a suburban home and a living room full of new furniture would provide happiness, and some felt this was not true. Friedan recommended that women delay marriage and childbearing and find interesting work outside the home.

The success of *The Feminine Mystique* prompted a national dialogue on women's issues and encouraged society to reassess its ideas about women's roles. Thrust into the national spotlight, Friedan used her newfound fame to found the National Organization for Women (NOW) in 1966, spearheading the fight for equal rights for women. She served as the first president of NOW until 1970.

patient statistics were not broken down by gender, a 1968 study found that women were two times more likely to use these drugs than men. Pharmaceutical drug use was so common, in fact, that in 1967 the best-selling rock group, the Rolling Stones, had a number-one hit with the song "Mother's Little Helper," whose title refers to the slang term used for tranquilizers and other drugs.

The Single, Independent Woman

Whereas the unhappy pill-popping housewife was one mainstream sixties stereotype, the carefree single girl was another. The idealized concept of the "perky" unmarried woman became fashionable after the publication of the controversial book *Sex and the Single Girl* by Helen Gurley Brown in 1962. Brown opened the book with these words:

> [Far] from being a creature to be pitied and patronized, the single girl is emerging as the newest glamour girl of our times. . . . When a man thinks of a married woman, no matter how lovely she is, he must inevitably picture her . . . fixing little children's lunches, or scrubbing them down because they've fallen in a mudhole. . . . When a man thinks of a single woman, he pictures her alone in her apartment, smooth legs sheathed in pink silk Capri pants, lying tantalizingly among dozens of satin cushions, trying to read but not very successfully, for HE is in the room—filling her thoughts, her dreams, her life.[9]

Sex and the Single Girl, which was made into a popular movie featuring Natalie Wood, shaped a generation of young women by preaching personal fulfillment through the use of makeup, fashion, exercise, and noncommittal relationships. As

Melissa Hantman writes in "Helen Gurley Brown" on Salon.com, Brown "prattled about the joys of women doing and having it all: excelling at work, splurging on luxuries, beguiling men. Decades before, ad execs had targeted women as leading consumers; now, Brown was urging her

Author Helen Gurley Brown, who encouraged single women's success, leans on a stack of books.

reader to snag a man (or men) to [satisfy] her physical, emotional and material appetites."[10]

Brown followed the success of her book by taking a job as editor in chief of *Cosmopolitan* magazine. In her first editor's column in 1965, Brown wrote that the magazine was for the "grown-up girl, interested in whatever can give you a richer, more exciting, fun-filled, friend-filled, man-loved kind of life!"[11]

Hantman describes *Cosmo*'s somewhat revolutionary content during the midsixties and the importance of the magazine in helping shape the role of the ideal single woman of the time:

> Brown exhorted ambition and assertiveness over [men], on dates or on the job. She repeatedly linked careers to single-woman prowess, and both monetary and emotional stability: "A single woman is known by what she does rather than whom she belongs to." . . . But even career advice upheld images and ideals of femininity . . . [such as] flirting with the management: A job "has everything to do with men anyway," Brown writes. In 1969, *Cosmo* reported on secretaries "who've made very, very good." Their tactics range from impressing the boss to marrying him. So who's in power—the exec who seduces, or the men who deliver? Why do women work—to meet men or outfox them? . . .

In a tempest-tossed era of liberation, [*Cosmopolitan*] . . . grappled with the times' conundrums: how single women should define themselves, wield their newfound rights to have sex and to work, and—most importantly—reconcile liberation with attraction and affection toward men. Beyond doubt, Brown waxes more liberal than the radical feminism that sought to [do away with] gender roles altogether. Nonetheless, she had precarious ground to tread: voicing women's real-life concerns within the often idealistic [Liberation] Movement. She gave her readers glamour and confidence to be women, in all their glory.[12]

Women in the Workplace

Brown's success was based on the fact that more and more women were seeking employment as the decade wore on. As early as 1964 nearly 23 million women, or 35 percent, worked outside the home. By 1970 that number had risen to 44 percent. Although more women were working, however, 75 percent were segregated into "female only" jobs such as secretaries, cooks, maids, and so on. And despite Brown's vision of work as a carefree steppingstone to happiness, pay was low: Women earned an average of sixty cents for every dollar earned by a man, and in

Sex and the Single Girl

❦

The institution of marriage was widely promoted by the media during the 1960s. But the tantalizing "single girl" also gained national notice in 1962 when Helen Gurley Brown published *Sex and the Single Girl*. The book, which quickly became a worldwide best-seller published in twenty-three countries, was full of fashion tips, decorating guidance, and dating advice. With chapters titled "When to Meet Him," "How to Be Sexy," "The Apartment," "The Wardrobe," and "The Affair: From Beginning to End," *Sex and the Single Girl* was full of tips, formulas, tricks, and tests to help single women negotiate the world of dating.

Years before the rise of feminism and "free love," Brown challenged the traditional concepts of love, marriage, and a woman's place in society. Brown encour-

aged single women to be independent, strive to achieve their dream careers, and have affairs without commitment.

Sex and the Single Girl laid the groundwork for Brown's next project—editing *Cosmopolitan* magazine. Simply known as *Cosmo,* the magazine promptly became an icon of the swinging 1960s single woman, or "Cosmo Girl." When not publishing shallow articles with titles such as "The Man-Trap Apartment," *Cosmo* presented well-written features by women authors such as Nora Ephron and Gael Greene. And unlike other magazines at the time that were written for general audiences, *Cosmo* was the first to focus on a well-defined segment of the population—the single working woman. As a result, readership soared, and Brown became the spokesperson for young, independent working women.

some fields, such as sales, women earned only forty cents to every dollar. This lower pay scale was meant to maintain a rigid cultural practice, as Fuentes writes: "Married women could work outside the home only if dire household finances required it. Under no circumstances were they to earn more money than their husbands."[13]

Some pointed out that women were paid less because they performed different work, but as Carol Hymowitz and

Michaele Weissman write in *A History of Women in America,* this was not always true:

The sexual division of work could be subtle. At times women and men performed work that was identical in all but name and salary. In insurance companies, both men and women processed policy applications, but the higher-paid men were called underwriters while the women were called raters.

One-third of the 1,900 office managers polled in 1961 admitted that they routinely paid men higher salaries than they paid to women in equivalent positions. Few saw anything wrong with the dual pay system. Women did not need as much money as men; and besides, they were worth less. Many businesses placed ceilings on the amount a female worker could earn. A woman who became "too expensive" was sometimes fired and replaced by a man.[14]

College-educated women did earn better salaries, but inequality with men's salaries remained. For example, a woman with a bachelor's degree was paid the same as a man with a high school diploma, and the average female worker was generally treated as an inferior no matter what her position. Grown women were referred to as *girls* and were often supervised as if they were schoolchildren. Hymowitz and Weissman quote one unnamed middle-aged woman's comments about her job at an insurance company:

[Women] were always treated like kids. If you got up from your desk you were told to sit down. If you looked around, you were told not to talk. If you went to the ladies' room too many times, they'd tell you. I was told they counted the papers in the wastepaper basket [to check for mistakes]. I did work with one woman who used to rip up the used papers, put them in her pocketbook, and flush them down the toilet.[15]

In some jobs, supervision did not end at the office door. Women who performed certain jobs, such as flight attendants, were expected to weigh a certain amount and were not even allowed to be married. A 1965 want ad by American Airlines revealed the strict criteria, calling for women who were between the ages of twenty and twenty-six, five foot two to five foot eight, under one hundred thirty pounds, and "single, in excellent health, attractive, and [possessing] considerable personal charm as well as a high degree of intelligence and enthusiasm."[16]

Working Mothers

Women who were mothers faced additional social pressure in the workplace. Throughout the sixties, most major corporations would not hire women with preschool children at home, a policy banned by the Supreme Court during the 1970s.

Women who were pregnant faced another set of obstacles. Until 1968 female educators in most states were not allowed to teach school during the last four months of pregnancy. And since employers did not want to train women only to have them leave if they became pregnant, some women were formally asked to discuss their contraception practices. In the book *In the Company of Women* by Bonnie Watkins and Nina Rothchild, banker Dianne E. Arnold describes how her private life was the subject of intense scrutiny:

[In 1966] I'd gone to a job fair, and First Bank was one of the companies I talked to there. They were one of those who quizzed me about my birth control practices—I was married at the time—which in retrospect just blows my mind. These starchy men sitting there asking me these outrageous questions![17]

Despite the discrimination, women were more in demand in the workplace as the decade progressed. Changes in technology required tens of thousands of new female workers to type data into primitive computing devices in the electronic data-processing industry. Women were also hired in the new fast-food industry, in which flexible hours and part-time work were important for those with children. And during the second half of the 1960s, hundreds of thousands of women were forced into the workplace when their husbands were drafted and sent to Vietnam.

Professional Women

Although women flooded into the low-wage sector of the economy, the numbers of female professionals remained low throughout the 1960s. By the end of the decade women made up only about 2 percent of the nation's architects, 3 percent of the lawyers, 7 percent of the physicians, and 9 percent of the scientists. Only in the teaching profession were women represented in larger numbers, making up a total of 22 percent of the faculties at colleges and universities. As June Sochen writes in *Herstory,* "The professions did not admit [women], the graduate schools did not encourage them, and indeed even elementary schools discouraged girls from seeking advanced education, programming them early on to accept their cultural role."[18] Women who did achieve success or recognition in their fields continued to face discrimination, and even denigration, in the media. According to Linden-Ward and Green, "When scientist Dorothy C. Hodgkin won a Nobel Prize in 1964 [for determining the structure of biochemical compounds], the *New York Times* headline announced 'Grandmother Wins Award.'"[19]

Some women who wanted to challenge discrimination in college admissions and employment hiring practices dreamed of becoming lawyers. But as former Minnesota state representative Ann Wynia writes,

One thing I remember from college was wanting to go to law school. But I knew a woman who was going to law

Sexism in the Sky

During the 1960s flight attendants were expected to follow strict guidelines that covered appearance and even marriage status. In an interview with Bonnie Watkins and Nina Rothchild for their book *In the Company of Women,* former flight attendant Linda Lavender Miller reveals that most women did not question their status until the years of women's liberation during the 1970s:

I went to work as a flight attendant. I was coming up against a lot of unfair stuff for women, but for some reason I wasn't able to compute it that way. We had to be unmarried, and if we got married we were without jobs. I never figured out until years later that they were using us to sell the airline, we were a commodity. What does it mean that you're unmarried? In those days, the great majority of passengers were male. The message was, "Not only do these women look good and do a nice job, but they're also available [for dating]. . . ."

Another thing was, the most senior flight attendant on the flight is the boss—seniority is everything. Your flight card always designated who was senior and who was junior, based, of course, on length of service. That was without exception, there was no way around it. *Unless* there was a male flight attendant on board—even if he started yesterday, he was in charge.

We had to weigh a certain amount, and the men didn't. When we came to work, we had to step on a scale. . . . If you were over the weight they had designated for you, you were laid off immediately without pay until you met your weight. . . . I ended up getting married unbeknownst to the airline, like we all did, and continuing to work. You had to be in charge of the phone when you were [at home] on reserve. If there was a guy answering the phone, you might be asked why he was there in the middle of the night.

Flight attendants pose for an airline ad, which presents women as a commodity of its flights.

school and the only goal she had was to become a legal secretary. I mean, this is . . . in the early '60s, and this is how a woman defined the limits of what they could do. I was interested in politics . . . [and] I remember thinking that I would like to marry a politician. This is how women thought about their options.[20]

The few women who were in the legal profession often found themselves handling less-prestigious "woman's work," such as wills, estates, and other family-based law. Others did the tedious work of researching and preparing cases for men who performed the more glamorous—and lucrative—work of arguing cases in court.

By the end of the decade, however, women began demanding equal rights under the law, and women lawyers were there to represent them. One such lawyer

Ruth Bader Ginsburg has served as a justice of the U.S. Supreme Court since 1993.

Women of the 1960s

was Ruth Bader Ginsburg, U.S. Supreme Court justice since 1993. Ginsburg well understood the sting of gender discrimination: While at Harvard during the 1950s, the dean asked the women of the class what it felt like to occupy places that could have gone to deserving men. When Ginsburg went on to teach at Rutgers in 1963, she was forced to hide her second pregnancy under baggy clothes to evade the university's ban on pregnant teachers. During the late 1960s, however, Ginsburg successfully argued, among several precedent-setting cases, for maternity leave rights for New Jersey schoolteachers. She later became the first director of the American Civil Liberties Union's Women's Rights Project. Ginsburg continued to argue her cases before men, however. Out of the ten thousand judges in the United States, only two hundred were women, and those were mostly in lower courts with limited powers.

Sweeping Changes

Although men outnumbered women in every profession, it only took a small percentage of women to instigate major changes in law, medicine, the sciences, journalism, and other areas. And the incremental rate by which these transformations were instituted began to gather dazzling speed after the decade drew to a close. By the end of the 1970s, the world of the working woman was changed almost beyond recognition with sexism and gender discrimination banned by law, custom, and company policy. Females continued to enter the workforce, and some young women began to plan careers as scientists, doctors, lawyers, business executives, and other professionals. In 1960 those plans would have been chided as daydreams. By the 1970s few women doubted their power to achieve such goals in a nation that had undergone a sweeping cultural metamorphosis.

Chapter 2:
Women Feminists

American women faced serious job discrimination throughout the 1960s. Beginning early in the decade, however, a high-level presidential commission spurred changes in federal law that helped promote gender equality in the workforce. With the law on its side, the fledgling women's liberation movement was able to rally its forces to break down well-entrenched gender barriers in social, business, and cultural situations. Events moved fast, and by the end of the decade a new generation of activist women began challenging traditional female roles on all levels, and lesbians and other minority groups promoted their particular political and social agendas.

The women's movement was first mobilized in 1961 when President John F. Kennedy created the blue-ribbon President's Commission on the Status of Women (PCSW). The executive order creating the commission listed the reasons such a panel was necessary:

> [Prejudices] and outmoded customs act as barriers to the full realization of women's basic rights which should be respected and fostered as part of our Nation's commitment to human dignity, freedom, and democracy. . . . [In] every period of national emergency women have served with distinction in widely varied capacities but thereafter have been subjected to treatment as a marginal group whose skills have been inadequately realized. . . . [A] Governmental Commission should be charged with the responsibility for developing recommendations for overcoming discriminations in government and private employment on the basis of sex and for developing recommendations for services which will enable women to continue their role as wives and mothers while making a maximum contribution to the world around them.[21]

The committee was chaired by the respected Eleanor Roosevelt, wife of former president Franklin Roosevelt. In order to avoid controversy, Roosevelt felt that priority should be given to the traditional female roles of wife and mother rather than to women in the workplace. As Roosevelt writes in "My Day—Women's Issues," on the American Experience website,

The effort, of course, is to find how we can best use the potentialities of women without impairing their first responsibilities, which are to their homes, their husbands and their

Feminist Leader Gloria Steinem

A s an author, activist, and founder of *Ms.* magazine, Gloria Steinem is one of the most renowned leaders of the feminist movement. As her biography on the "Women's History Month" website shows, her 1960s exposé of life as a Playboy bunny helped strengthen her feminist beliefs:

Gloria Steinem was born on March 25, 1934, in Toledo, Ohio. . . . She was the granddaughter of the noted suffragette, Pauline Steinem. Given her family's background, it was not surprising that she became a feminist and a journalist. . . .

In 1960 she moved to New York and began writing freelance articles for popular magazines. . . . One of her first major assignments in investigative journalism was a two-part series . . . on the working conditions of Playboy bunnies. In order to do research for the article, Steinem applied for a job as a Playboy bunny and was hired. She held the position for three weeks in order to do research. The articles that she wrote as a result of her experience exposed the poor working

conditions and meager wages of the women who worked long hours in the lavish clubs where rich men spent their leisure time. . . .

Steinem's feminist concerns were [further] sparked when she went to a meeting of the Redstockings, a New York women's liberation group. Although she went as a journalist with the intention of writing a story about the group, she found herself deeply moved by the stories the women told, particularly of the dangers of illegal abortions. . . .

By the late 1960s Steinem had gained national attention as an outspoken leader of the women's liberation movement, which continued to grow and gain strength. . . . [In] 1972 Steinem . . . gained funding for the first mass circulation feminist magazine, *Ms.* The preview issue sold out, and within five years *Ms.* had a circulation of 500,000. As editor of the magazine Steinem gained national attention as a feminist leader and became an influential spokesperson for women's rights issues.

children. We need to use in the very best way possible all our available manpower—and that includes womanpower—and this commission, I think, can well point out some of the ways in which this can be accomplished.[22]

A Defining Moment

Members of the PCSW included educators, writers, leaders of women's organizations, union leaders, five Kennedy cabinet members, and members of both houses of Congress. To perform its work, the commission was divided into seven subcommittees that studied issues such as maternity leave, employment, images of women in the mass media, and special problems faced by black women. Controversial topics such as birth control, abortion, and female poverty were purposely and conspicuously ignored.

The PCSW issued a report in October 1963 with a number of proposals that could be followed by institutions and governments to alleviate gender bias.

John F. Kennedy meets with PCSW chairperson Eleanor Roosevelt (left) to discuss the status of women in society.

These recommendations included making admission requirements to colleges more flexible in order to admit more women; encouraging privately funded child-care centers for working mothers; providing paid maternity leave; expanding job-counseling services for women; and ending gender-based hiring and job discrimination practices within the federal government.

At the time the PCSW made these recommendations, it represented a defining moment in women's history. This was the first time that the federal government had launched an investigation into the status of women and their roles in society. And with an official presidential report in hand, women's groups now had proof that changes were necessary. As Friedan writes, "The very existence of the PCSW . . . creates a climate where it is possible to recognize and do something about the discrimination against women in terms not only of pay but of the subtle barriers to opportunity."[23]

In addition to laying the groundwork for a national referendum on gender issues, several members of the PCSW continued their work in the women's movement during later years. Pauli Murray, who went on to become a founding member of the National Organization for Women (NOW), describes how her work with the commission opened her eyes to gender discrimination, saying that she experienced

Pauli Murray fought for women's rights as a member of PCSW and later as a founding member of NOW.

a "high level consciousness-raising . . . because it was the first time in my life that I really sat down and researched the status of women."[24]

State Commissions

Perhaps the most important recommendation of the PCSW—and the one with the most wide-ranging influence—was that each state form similar commissions to study local problems. By 1964, 32 states had established such panels, and by 1967, all 50 states had done so. (Today there are approximately 270 state, county, and local commissions for women in the United States and its territories.)

With each state and many cities establishing such commissions, thousands of women found new roles for themselves as spokespersons for their gender in a political world dominated almost entirely by men. Women on state commissions compiled bias statistics and testified before political committees in order to change laws and advance women's causes. To raise funds, they spoke to women's social groups and other organizations, educating the public about sexist practices confronting women.

In Minnesota, Edna L. Schwartz was appointed to the state's Commission on the Status of Women when it was established in 1964. According to Schwartz, the committee operated on the slimmest of budgets but was able to garner much attention in the press:

We never had any money, we had no [political] support, we had nothing. We just begged. We would go out and speak [to various organizations] about [equal rights] or equal pay, and we'd [raise] maybe $5. We used the money for printing, to do reports. . . .

[But we] were so enthused. We were so sure that this was going to solve all the problems, if we could just get everybody to know about all this. We got a lot of coverage [in newspapers]. I got clippings, and we got our pic-

ture in the paper, oh my goodness. Why, you'd have thought someone like myself was a celebrity. . . .

We were taken quite seriously.[25]

Mandating Equal Opportunity

While women were setting up commissions in various states, Congress passed the Equal Pay Act, which established equal pay for men and women performing the same job duties. Although equal pay became the law of the land, women continued to be denied equivalent compensation throughout the sixties. But as Leila J. Rupp and Verta Taylor write in *Survival in the Doldrums,* "It represented a significant first step towards winning the government's commitment to eliminating gender-based discrimination. As a result, the passage of the bill . . . focused attention on women's issues and brought together women from government, labor, and women's organizations."[26]

This synergy between various women's organizations helped motivate Congress to pass the Civil Rights Act of 1964. Although aimed at eliminating discrimination against African Americans, title 7 of the act specifically bars employment discrimination on the basis of sex. The bill also established the five-member Equal Employment Opportunity Commission (EEOC) to hear complaints from people who believed they had faced discrimination in the workplace.

The EEOC established guidelines that said an employer could not prefer a man over a woman, but few employers felt obligated to follow these new laws. This is demonstrated by the fact that the EEOC fielded over fifty thousand complaints of gender discrimination before 1970.

Although most members of the EEOC felt their main duty was to fight racial discrimination, the commission quickly became a forum on sex discrimination in the workplace, as the first female lawyer on the EEOC, Sonia Pressman Fuentes, recalls:

President Lyndon B. Johnson shakes hands with Dr. Martin Luther King Jr., after signing the Civil Rights Act.

In the Commission's first fiscal year, about 37 percent of the complaints alleged sex discrimination, and these complaints raised a host of new issues that were more difficult than those raised by the complaints of race discrimination. Could employers continue to advertise in classified advertising columns headed "Help Wanted—Male" and "Help Wanted—Female"? Did they have to hire women for jobs traditionally reserved for men? Could airlines continue to ground or fire stewardesses when they married or reached the age of thirty-two or thirty-five? What about state protective laws that prohibited the employment of women in certain occupations, limited the number of hours they could work and the amount of weight they could lift, and required certain benefits for them, such as seats and rest periods? Did school boards have to keep teachers on after they became pregnant? What would students think if they saw pregnant teachers? Wouldn't they know they'd had sexual intercourse? Did employers have to provide the same pensions to men and women even though women as a class outlived men?[27]

Though the EEOC faced the daunting task of redefining the traditional roles played by women in the workplace, it also inspired women to challenge less serious problems. For example, a common grievance of female college students was the lack of women's bathrooms in some school buildings designed primarily for male students. In 1965 biophysicist Phyllis Kahn, who later became a Minnesota state legislator, was inspired by the creation of the EEOC to do something about this situation. Recently drawn to feminist activism, Kahn used humor to shame the university into adding women's rest rooms to a new building:

> One of the first things I did concerned a new building being built, a new science building [at the University of Minnesota]. A couple of us discovered that it had no women's rooms. So another woman and I wrote a paper about it—it was like a scientific paper, a spoof—with tables and data and all that. We showed how women needed more bathrooms than men, not less. We did it as a draft copy, and copies went everywhere. To the president of the university, to the EEOC, to the congressmen, to the newspaper. The dean wasn't happy, but they did change the building.[28]

Despite such small victories, the EEOC was dominated by men who were adamantly opposed to equal rights for women. As Fuentes continued to challenge

The Women's Bill of Rights

In November 1967 the National Organization for Women ratified its Women's Bill of Rights, a document that addressed many problems facing average American women. It was reprinted in *The Times Were a Changin'*, edited by Irwin and Debi Unger.

WE DEMAND:

I. That the U.S. Congress immediately pass the Equal Rights Amendment to the Constitution to provide that "Equality of rights under the law shall not be denied or abridged by the United States or by any state on account of sex." . . .

II. That equal employment opportunity be guaranteed to all women. . . .

III. That women be protected by law to ensure their rights to return to their jobs within a reasonable time after childbirth without loss of seniority . . . and be paid maternity leave. . . .

IV. Immediate revision of tax laws to permit the deduction of home and child-care expenses for working parents.

V. That child-care facilities be established by law on the same basis as parks, libraries, and public schools, adequate to the needs of children. . . .

VI. That the right of women to be educated to their full potential equally with men be secured by federal and state legislation, eliminating all discrimination and segregation by sex . . . at all levels of education, including colleges, graduate and professional schools, loans and fellowships, and federal and state training programs such as the Job Corps.

VII. The right of women in poverty to secure job training, housing, and family allowances on equal terms with men . . . [and] revision of welfare legislation and poverty programs which deny women dignity, privacy, and self-respect.

VIII. The right of women to control their own reproductive lives by removing from the penal code laws limiting access to contraceptive information and devices, and by repealing penal laws governing abortion.

NOW chairman of the board Dr. Kathryn F. Clarenbach (left) and president Betty Friedan are pictured.

this attitude in an often hostile environment, she began to question her own role on the commission, writing,

> I became *the* staff person who stood for aggressive enforcement of the sex discrimination prohibitions of the Act, and this caused me no end of grief. At the end of one day, after a particularly frustrating discussion . . . I left the EEOC building with tears streaming down my face. I didn't know how I had gotten into this position—fighting for women's rights. No one had elected me to represent women. Why was I engaged in this battle against men who had power where I had none?[29]

The National Organization for Women

Fuentes soon found that she was not alone and that other women were angry that complaints filed with the EEOC did little to change deeply engrained attitudes in society. In 1966, after the success of her book *The Feminine Mystique,* Betty Friedan founded an organization to utilize the EEOC to challenge sex discrimination in the courts.

Friedan and twenty-eight other women (including Fuentes) each contributed $5 as a seed fund for the National Organization for Women. With this tiny startup budget, the group quickly raised more money, and before the year was out, NOW had set up

seven task forces to study the roles of women in society: family life, education, employment, media, religion, women in poverty, and women's legal and political rights.

The organization was also concerned with the harm done by stereotypical roles of weak, helpless, or brainless women portrayed in the media and public institutions. This was explained in the NOW Statement of Purpose, issued in 1966:

> We will protest and endeavor to change the false image of women now prevalent in the mass media and in the texts, ceremonies, laws and practices of our major social institutions . . . church, state, college, factory or office which in the guise of protectiveness . . . foster in women self-denigration, dependence and evasion of responsibility, [and] undermine their confidence in their own abilities and foster contempt for women.[30]

By 1967 NOW was formally incorporated, with offices in Washington, D.C. Thanks to NOW lobbying, President Lyndon B. Johnson signed a bill that prohibited sex discrimination in employment by the federal government and by contractors doing business with the government.

While wielding a growing power in Washington, members of NOW were forced to confront discrimination in everyday life. This was clearly demonstrated at a 1967 meeting at the Hotel Biltmore in

Outside the White House, members of NOW protest for the passage of the Equal Rights Amendment.

New York City. After a tedious day of conferences and discussion groups, many of the women were ready to have a drink in the hotel bar. But when the thirsty women arrived at the nearly empty Biltmore Men's Bar and Grill, they were refused service because it was a men-only establishment, common at that time in cities throughout the country.

After the angry women returned to the meeting room, they had a discussion, as Friedan recalls in her book *It Changed My Life:* "I mean, it's the height of ridiculousness to be sitting here pretending to be an organization to end sex discrimination and shut our eyes to it in the very hotel we're meeting in."[31]

The women notified media that they were going to stage a sit-in—that is, occupy the bar and refuse to leave until they were served. But when they arrived, the bar was closed and its door was padlocked. Apparently one of the husbands who was attending the meeting had disagreed with the action and notified the management, which promptly closed the bar. But the media arrived in time to film the women protesting in front of the closed bar.

Protesting Miss America

The women's movement gained national attention on September 7, 1968, when about two hundred women from several organizations, including the New York Radical Women and WITCH (Women's International Terrorist Conspiracy from Hell), protested in front of the Miss America Pageant in Atlantic City, New Jersey. The Radical Women brought a sheep to the pageant to symbolize the mindless and docile image of women that beauty contests represented.

During the festivities protesters set off stink bombs inside the pageant hall. While authorities were attending to this diversion, protesters began chanting "Freedom for women" and "No more Miss America."

The demonstrators also held up a huge banner that read "WOMEN'S LIBERATION." Camera operators inside the pageant focused on the banner, and this statement suddenly flashed across television sets throughout the world. It was the first time this mysterious phrase had ever been seen by the public at large, and few knew what it meant until it was explained in newspapers the next day.

Meanwhile, outside the pageant, protesters set up a "freedom trash can," an item that soon became a regular icon at women's protest rallies. The trash can was there for women to toss their makeup, false eyelashes, dish towels, copies of *Playboy* and *Cosmopolitan,* and a few padded brassieres—items that were perceived to enforce stereotypical gender roles assigned by society.

Although women did not burn any undergarments at the Miss America Pageant, a journalist falsely reported that a burning bra was thrown in the freedom trash can. Several weeks later a Chicago disk jockey paid three attractive fashion models to throw a few burning bras into a trash can. This staged event was filmed, and the footage was shown repeatedly across the country. Since that time, the concept of "bra-burning feminists" became an entrenched myth in American culture.

The protest by the New York Radical Women garnered more attention than the Miss America Pageant itself, however, and this demonstration became the prototype for other protests staged by women at the end of the sixties.

Feminists protest the Miss America Pageant in 1968.

This inspired women across the country to take up the role of protester. In Pittsburgh women sat-in at the expensive Stouffer's grill, and as Friedan writes, they "even invaded the superjock McSorleys Old Ale House."[32] These headline-grabbing actions quickly forced politicians to do something, and within months, New York, Pennsylvania, and several other eastern states passed bills to end gender discrimination in public restaurants and bars.

Changing Lives on a Local Level

Large organizations like NOW galvanized women to spontaneously start their own grassroots political groups throughout the country in order to seek change on a local level. And the concept of small neighborhood women's groups spread across the country with amazing speed, their existence promoted mainly by word of mouth. This experience was recalled by author and history professor Sara M. Evans:

Somebody came by [my house] and said, "There's a group of women been meeting for a month or so, don't you want to come?" I was there, and I don't remember having a moment of doubt about it. It was a real easy slide. And that's how I fell into one of the very first women's liberation groups in the country, in 1967.

We just called our group "Women's Liberation." Later the groups proliferated rapidly and we had to give names to things, so we called it the [Chicago] "West Side Group." Soon there were other groups and I was going to all of them. That year was incredibly transforming for me. The women's movement became fundamental to my identity. . . . But we didn't want to just exchange ideas. We were about changing the world.[33]

While women's organizations in big cities, such as the West Side Group, were planning change on a grand scale, the movement even spread to the suburbs, where women were coming together to talk, share experiences, and make important decisions about their lives. As Mary Ziegenhagen, the first woman editor for the *Minneapolis Star,* recalls,

In my own neighborhood, out in the suburbs, there were a couple of ongoing [women's groups]. But usually they only lasted five or six times. Then women would more or less decide what they were going to do. Some of them got divorces, some of them went to college, some of them had another baby, some of them ran for school board. They didn't need much. People were ready to move, and all they needed was any teeny little group that would say, "Good for you, go do it."[34]

One of the missions taken on by the women's groups was to end sex discrimination in want ads, which were separated into "Help Wanted—Male" and "Help Wanted—Female" categories. This was an issue because higher-paying jobs in management and professional fields were listed under the male column while "pink-collar" jobs such as housekeeping, clerical work, counter sales, and other traditionally female occupations were listed in the female section.

In Minneapolis, Katherine Weesner founded Women Against Male Superiority (WAMS) to protest segregated want ads at the *Minneapolis Star.* After picketing for many months, WAMS took direct action, as Weesner recalls:

We made stickers that said "Stop Sexigated Want Ads." They were sticky stickers. So we went one night and climbed over the . . . fence of the newspaper and pasted these stickers on the windshields of their trucks, at one o'clock in the morning. So when the papers were ready to load onto the trucks, they had to delay it to get the stickers off.

Of course there weren't any stories about any of this in the newspaper. But we had another meeting after that. Finally the manager of the classified ads said, "We're going to change it. But we're not just doing this

because it's a sign of the times." . . . Some people reacted after it was changed. Some women were angry, because now they didn't know which jobs they could apply for. They said, "It's a waste of our time applying for jobs we're not going to get"—which was true.[35]

Changing Roles at Home

While women were marching in the streets to protest the sexist practices of newspapers and other institutions, it was unavoidable that they would begin challenging the roles of housewife and mother that they often assumed at home. And the confrontations between men and women, husbands and wives, might have been just as tense as those between police and protesters. The challenges facing couples were outlined by Pat Mainardi in an essay titled "The Politics of Housework," published by Redstockings, a women's liberation group in New York City:

A great many American men are not accustomed to doing monotonous, repetitive work which never issues in any lasting, let alone important, achievement. This is why they would rather repair a cabinet than wash dishes. If human endeavors are like a pyramid with man's highest achievements at the top, then keeping oneself alive is at the bottom. Men have always had servants (us) to take care of this bottom stratum of life while they have confined their efforts to the rarefied upper regions.[36]

The National Organization for Women also wanted to change the roles of men, asking husbands to join their wives in caring for children and performing housework. As it wrote in the NOW Statement of Purpose,

We believe that a true partnership between the sexes demands a different concept of marriage, an equitable sharing of the responsibilities of home and children and of the economic burdens of their support. We believe that proper recognition should be given to the economic and social values of homemaking and child care.[37]

When women tried to challenge the long-standing roles of men and women at home, however, they quickly learned that most men had little interest in changing their roles. As Mainardi writes, "He is feeling it more than you. He's losing some leisure and you're gaining it. The measure of your oppression is his resistance."[38]

The Rise of Radical Women

Many women who analyzed the roles played by men and women in relationships began to challenge the entire concept of marriage, housekeeping, and child-bearing. By the end of the decade some women were so radicalized that they were ready to do away with matrimony, heterosexual sex, and even men themselves. This caused a great rift between younger women, who came of age during often violent antiwar protests, and older, more moderate feminists in organizations such as NOW, which was founded to advocate slow and steady change within the system, using the courts and Congress to enforce laws that guaranteed equality. As Friedan writes in *It Changed My Life,*

We can change institutions but it is a fantasy deviation from a really revolutionary approach to say that we want a world in which there will be no sex, no marriage, that in order for women to be free they must have a manless revolution and down with men. . . . We have to deal with the world of reality if we are going to have a real revolution. . . . [Don't] tell me that anybody can [imagine] a possible revolution . . . if it says, "We're going to kill off the men and refuse to breed male babies."[39]

Despite Friedan's attempt to promote unity within the women's liberation movement, it was typical of the era that the movement soon splintered into several factions during the last years of the sixties.

Radical feminists believed that racism, the Vietnam War, American domination of smaller countries, and other broad political issues were a logical extension of men's power over women. As the Redstockings women's group explained in the 1969 Redstockings manifesto, "Male supremacy is the oldest and most basic form of domination . . . and model for all other forms of oppression . . . including racism and capitalism and thus the tapeworm that must be eliminated first by any true revolution. Men dominate women, a few men dominate the rest."[40]

Radical feminist groups also rejected the centralized control of NOW and preferred to meet in small "cooperatives" in which traditional roles were abandoned. For example, some groups banned leaders and preferred to share all jobs, including such bones of contention as making coffee, cleaning, and secretarial work. In the decades before the Internet, the loose network of feminists communicated via newsletters, journals, and conferences.

When the most traditional roles of a woman's life were called into question, it was said that the "personal became political." In the 1960s many women came to see basic features of their physical appearance and demeanor as political statements, as Sally Kempton writes in "Cutting Loose," an article in *Esquire* magazine:

There is often a sense of genuine cultural rebellion in the atmosphere of a Woman's Liberation meeting. Women sit with their legs apart, carelessly dressed, barely made up, exhibiting their feelings or the holes on the knees of their jeans with an unprovocative candor which is hardly seen at all in the outside world. Of course, they are demonstrating by their postures that they are in effect, off duty, absolved from the compulsion of making themselves attractive.[41]

Lesbian Feminists

The growth of women's liberation was accompanied by the 1960s sexual revolution, in which women began to question traditional sexual roles and experiment not only with premarital and extramarital sex but also with taboo practices such as bisexual and homosexual sex. This inspired thousands of homosexual women, or lesbians, to "come out of the closet" and celebrate their sexual orientation openly for the first time. Many of these women were attracted to the women's liberation movement because, as Marilyn Barrow writes, "as Lesbians we are . . . in the sand hole; we are women (itself a . . . minority status) and we are Lesbians; the last half of the least noticed, most disadvantaged minority."[42]

Although their role was downplayed by relatively conservative groups such as NOW, many lesbians were involved in the feminist movement. The reasons are explained by David Farber in *The Great Age of Dreams*:

A woman holds a placard for the Gay Liberation Front, which contributed to the women's liberation movement.

For a committed radical feminist, dedicated to fighting women's dependence on men, at its root, lesbianism made a certain amount of ideological sense. In addition, the women's liberation movement really did attract the support of many lesbians, who without husbands to rely on for econom-

ic support, had more reason than most straight women to actively pursue gender equality.[43]

Although gay rights and radical feminism remained controversial and alienated many Americans, the basic ideas behind the women's movement were difficult for anyone to refute: Discrimination was wrong whether it was based on a person's religion, race, or gender. That some women reacted to it more angrily than others was a sign of the times during an angry decade that saw wars, riots, assassinations, and revolution in the streets. By 1970 NOW had more than three hundred thousand members with chapters in every state. Dozens of best-selling books and hundreds of magazine articles had exposed almost everyone in the country to feminist theory.

In cities and suburbs across the country women formed "consciousness-raising groups" in which they could meet and discuss the personal details of their lives. At these sessions women often discovered that they had much in common. For the first time, women were able to openly discuss personal tragedies such as physical and sexual abuse or rape. As these problems were brought out into the open, support and counseling groups were formed, and women were able to seek help where none had ever been available before. As the ideas behind the feminist movement gained national prominence, terms such as *sexist* and *male chauvinist* joined the American lexicon.

The 1960s had started as a decade in which the large majority of women assumed the roles of mothers and housewives. In ten short years, however, the roles that women had been assigned for centuries were called into question and oftentimes abandoned. The effect this had on women is described by Phyllis Chesler in *Women and Madness:*

> Some women quit their jobs . . . others began job training. . . . Some women started living together, some began living alone for the first time. . . . Some women left their husbands, others began to live with a man, feeling somehow less of a psychological disadvantage than before. Many women started reading "political" and "scientific" books as passionately as they read novels. . . . Women stopped giggling and competing with each other for male attention. . . . Many women found they could think. . . . Some women stopped going to beauty parlors. . . . They began to value their time; they needed fewer adornments to "make up" for being female.[44]

Addressing gender discrimination would lead many newly minted feminists to addressing racial discrimination as well, in the turbulent civil rights movement of the decade.

Chapter 3:
Women in the Civil Rights Movement

The women's liberation movement was founded by mothers, housewives, lawyers, authors, doctors, and women who performed a host of other occupations. These women faced sexism and discrimination because of their gender. But a large percentage of these women were white, and most of them lived in middle- or even upper-class households. These feminists were often portrayed in the press as pampered housewives or spoiled suburban mothers.

African American women in the 1960s, however, were overwhelmingly poor. In fact, many of them cooked and cleaned for minimum wage in the homes of national women's liberation movement leaders. These black women faced extra hardships: Not only did they encounter prejudice because of their race, but they were also discriminated against because of their gender. As civil rights leader Mary Church Terrell said, "We labor under the double handicap of race and sex."[45] Even powerful male African American leaders failed to see the abilities of black women,

as Malcolm X wrote in his autobiography: "[The] true nature of man is to be strong, and a woman's true nature is to be weak, and while a man must at all times respect his woman, at the same time he needs to understand that he must control her if he expects to get her respect."[46]

In the 1960s the goals of feminism and the civil rights movement often overlapped, and women, black and white, worked to extend equal rights to African Americans.

Poverty and Discrimination

A large majority of African American women lived below the poverty line during the 1960s. Those who lived in big cities found that they had been abandoned by taxpayers as most middle-class whites moved to the suburbs in the 1950s, where segregation was the rule. Grocery stores in black neighborhoods were boarded up, parks fell to ruin, and conditions and performance in city schools sank. Sociologists noted the increasing fragmentation of black American families in inner cities. More and more, the feeding, tending, and education of children in the inner city fell to women, who were directly affected by these substandard conditions.

Those who could afford to leave the inner city faced open discrimination when they tried to move into the new suburbs. David Farber writes about the Long Island suburb of Levittown outside of New York City:

In 1960, 82,000 people lived in Long Island's Levittown, the most celebrated of the new suburban subdevelopments, and not one of them was African-American. Black families were told by the developers openly not to bother trying to buy a home—they were not welcome. Racial segregation, in the North and West, as well as in the

African American children play in the inner city, where living conditions were extremely poor in 1968.

Women of the 1960s

South, was a well accepted fact of life in the new suburbs.[47]

Work and Welfare

Faced with expensive, overcrowded, and rundown housing and the costs of child care, black women looked for work, but Farber lists the bleak job prospects for African American women in 1960:

[In] the South no African Americans [male or female] held political office, no blacks worked as lawyers, doctors, engineers, or executives in white-owned businesses or firms. [In February 1960 in] the *Atlanta Constitution,* in its race- and gender-segregated want ads . . . African-American women saw six listings for maids, and openings for a salad [preparation] girl, a laundress, and a babysitter.[48]

Black women who found jobs were often paid substandard wages; black women earned an average of only about forty-five cents for every dollar made by white males at comparative jobs. And many jobs performed by black women, such as suburban maids and restaurant workers, required them to commute on buses and trains for hours to get to and from work.

Facing such hardships, many black mothers relied on a form of welfare known as Aid to Families with Dependent Children. Even though government checks helped millions to survive, only mothers with minor children but no husband qualified to receive it. In effect, critics claimed, welfare discouraged marriage, encouraged out-of-wedlock childbirth, and created a generation of children whose fathers were not at home. Black women were the primary recipients: Although black women made up 12 percent of the population, they composed 50 percent of the female-headed households in America.

Conditions for black women were particularly harsh in the southern states, where blatant discrimination was widespread. They were denied such basic rights as eating at lunch counters, shopping in department stores, and voting. In *Too Heavy a Load,* Deborah Gray White lists the many ways that prejudice and discrimination hurt black women and why the civil rights movement grew to such prominence during the decade:

Segregation, with its prohibitions against trying on clothes in the store fitting rooms and using public restrooms, denied black women basic dignity. Finding ways of telling hungry children why they could not eat or drink at restaurants and soda fountains was almost as trying as riding the segregated buses that extended the oppression of the black domestic's workday. In fact, because most black women had to work, and usually worked at the dirtiest, hardest, lowest paying jobs, any change the movement brought in black employment, whether for men or women, improved the black women's economic wellbeing. . . . In short, the Civil Rights movement promised to meet many black female needs and demands. To work for the race was to work for black women.[49]

Women at the Sit-Ins

African Americans began to protest lunch counter segregation on February 1, 1960, when four neatly dressed black college students entered the Woolworth's department store in Greensboro, South Carolina. The store had a lunch counter that catered to whites only, and as Zita Allen writes in *Black Women Leaders of the Civil Rights Movement,* this was an "inhumane and humiliating daily [reminder] of the belief that blacks were inferior to whites."[50] When the students sat down and ordered coffee, the waitress refused to serve them. They sat quietly at the counter until the store closed an hour later. The next day, twenty black students, both male and female, sat at the lunch counter. On the third day, sixty students were refused service.

As these students sat-in at the lunch counter, they were taunted and harassed by a crowd of white men who gathered behind them. Photos show female college students at sit-ins showered with broken eggs, hot coffee, ketchup, and lit cigarettes while police watched from a distance. Despite this abuse, hundreds of women took on the role of peaceful protester as lunch counter sit-ins spread to sixty-eight cities in the following months. An early protester, Ruby Doris Smith, recalls her experience in Georgia:

I began to think right away about [a sit-in] happening in Atlanta, but I wasn't ready to act on my own. When the student committee was formed at the Atlanta University Center, I [signed up] on the list. And when 200 students were selected for the first demonstration, I was among them. I went through the food line in the restaurant at the State Capitol with six other students but when we got to the cashier, she wouldn't take our money. She ran upstairs to the Governor. The Lieutenant-Governor came down and told us to leave. We didn't and went to the county jail.[51]

Women who were jailed were often strip-searched—and sometimes raped—by white male police officers, and conditions in jail cells often were appalling. But the courage and dedication of these women who swelled the ranks of sit-in protesters quickly paid off. Widespread public pressure and negative publicity forced the gov-

Four young men protest a whites-only lunch counter at Woolworth's department store.

ernment into action, and within months southern lunch counters were integrated.

Strong Women, Strong Leaders

The Greensboro sit-in inspired Ella Baker, a longtime civil rights leader, to found the Student Nonviolent Coordinating Committee (SNCC), one organization in which women composed the majority of members. As one member stated, "It's no secret that young people and women led organizationally."[52]

Baker had previously worked in the Southern Christian Leadership Conference (SCLC) founded by Martin Luther King Jr., but she quit the male-dominated civil rights organization because she disagreed with the SCLC policy of strong central leadership over grassroots organization. Within the SNCC, every person played an important role because, as Baker said, "strong people don't need strong leaders."[53] Professor of history and African American studies Charles Payne explains how this attitude influenced the SNCC:

Ella Baker, founder of SNCC, speaks at a press conference in 1968.

SNCC was the most active organization in the [Mississippi] Delta and it was relatively open to women.... [In] SNCC's early years, women were always involved in the development of policy and the execution of the group's program. The group was ... willing to work with anyone who was willing to have them, traditional considerations of status notwithstanding. They worked with sharecroppers as well as doctors, with the pool room crowd as well as the church crowd.

SNCC organizers emphasized finding and developing nontraditional sources of leadership. Women obviously represented an enormous pool of untapped leadership potential. Much of SNCC's organizing activity in the Delta involved door-to-door canvassing, which meant that women were as likely as men to encounter organizers. SNCC, despite the traditional definitions of sex roles held by many of its members, was structurally open to female participation in a way that many older organizations were not. Had SNCC employed a more traditional style of organizing—working primarily through previously established leadership—it might not have achieved the degree of female participation it did.[54]

In addition to being "woman-friendly," the SNCC was also a young organization, with 75 percent of its field workers under the age of twenty-two. And this idealistic organization quickly became the proving ground for a new generation of black female activists.

Diane Nash was one such leader. After she was arrested for participating in a sit-in in South Carolina, Nash refused to pay bail, instead volunteering, along with Ruby Doris Smith and nine male protesters, to serve thirty days in prison instead. The idea of Nash's insistence on "jail-no-bail" swept through the sit-in movement, and soon southern prisons were overflowing with protesters, creating a huge workload for guards and police officers who had to tend to their basic needs. Nash, who was pregnant at the time of her arrest, stated her reasons for adopting this uncompromising attitude:

The time has come for us to mean what we say and stop posting [bail]. This will be a black baby born in Mississippi and thus, wherever it is born, it will be born in prison. I believe that if I go to jail now it will help hasten that day when my child and all children will be free—not only on the day of their birth but for all their lives.[55]

Challenging Male Leadership

While SNCC members like Nash played an important role in the broad civil rights movement, groups such as the National Council of Negro Women (NCNW) focused on the effects of racism on women.

Dorothy Height, the leader of the NCNW, felt it was important to have a women's organization involved with the civil rights movement so that gender-specific issues such as child care, women's employment, and sexism would not be overshadowed by desegregation and black voting rights. As Height says,

I found that it was very difficult to get people, who are oriented towards [changing] laws and practices like [segregation] to accept the fact that conditions affecting children, and affecting youth, and affecting women, whether they were services like child care, or whether they were things related to employment opportunities . . . was all part of civil rights.[56]

In 1963, when the SCLC organized what would become the historic March on Washington featuring King's "I Have a Dream" speech, Height and others began to question the role of women in the mainstream civil rights movement. When women confronted the male leadership on this issue, they were largely ignored. As Height writes in *Sisters in the Struggle,*

There was an all-consuming focus on race. We women were expected to put all our energies into it. Clearly, there was a low tolerance level for anyone raising the questions about the women's participation. . . . The men seemed to feel that women were digressing and pulling the discussion off the main track. But it wasn't just a male attitude. There were black women who felt that we needed to stick with the "real" issue of race. It was thought that we were making a lot of fuss about an insignificant issue, that we did not recognize that the

Facing Down the Racists

Women who fought for civil rights in the South risked their lives for their beliefs. Even attempting to buy dinner in a restaurant could turn into a harrowing experience. In *Too Heavy a Load,* Deborah Gray White recalls an incident involving civil rights leader Dorothy Height in 1964:

> Dorothy Height . . . and two other black women went to a motel restaurant in Jackson [Mississippi]. As she recalled, events took a mean turn the minute they took their seats. First, the waitress gave them the cold shoulder, and soon they were approached by the owner, who

Civil rights leader Dorothy Height often risked her life.

bombarded the middle-aged women with questions:"What are you girls doing here? Where are you from? You must be from out of town." It only infuriated him to discover that one of Height's companions was local. "You must know how dangerous it is for you to be in here. You know that your people are not supposed to be coming in here!" he yelled. One by one the white patrons left the restaurant and were replaced by uniformed white [police] men who closed in on Height and her friends as they waited for dinner. As Height's mind raced to find a way out, one of her companions moved nervously toward a phone to call for help. Suddenly, Height noticed that the restaurant was slowly filling with black kitchen help who pretended to clean tables, while keeping watchful eyes on them. Somewhat relieved but still frightened, Height and her companions paid for their untouched meal and left. On their way out a uniformed white man scowled, "You know that you are not supposed to be in here." Relieved to escape this life-threatening situation, Height and her companions breathed even easier when they exited to find that all of the black men employed at the motel were lined up to form a protective corridor for them from the restaurant to the parking lot.

March was about racism, not sexism. We knew all that. But, we made it clear that we wanted to hear from at least one woman in the March dealing with jobs and freedom. We knew, firsthand, that most of the Civil Rights Movement audiences were largely comprised of women, children, and youth.[57]

Eventually the women agreed to put the issue aside temporarily, on the condition that at least one woman would be a featured speaker at the event. Even this request was denied. As a concession, women were allowed to sit on the stage, which was usually dominated by men. This angered some women in the movement, including Pauli Murray, who later said that the male leadership had the "tendency to assign women to a secondary, ornamental, or 'honoree' role instead of the partnership role in the civil rights movement which they have earned by their courage, intelligence, and dedication."[58]

In the months that followed, Height continued to challenge the male power structure of the civil rights movement. The NCNW held a meeting called "After the March, What?" at which black women discussed their roles in the movement and how they could best achieve their goals of gender and racial equality. Their concerns were largely unanswered by other major civil rights groups, however.

Despite the fact that women's issues were not addressed at that time, Height and others continued to support the important work done by the SCLC in matters of race. The March on Washington had galvanized the nation to enforce equal rights for African Americans and pushed Congress to pass the 1964 Civil Rights Act barring discrimination on account of race. And although women were denied vocal representation at the march, Height noted its positive effects:

> [The] March on Washington experience . . . brought into bold relief the different perspectives of men and women on the whole issue of gender. Though every statistic showed us that a number of our families were headed by women, we were still dominated by the view that if men were given enough, the women would be better off. There was not that sense of equal partnership. For many of us, the March opened that sense of equal partnership. For many of us, the March opened up the dialogue. It made it necessary. We had to talk about it.[59]

Fighting for Voting Rights

The NCNW was active in many areas of the civil rights movement and worked with other mainstream organizations. During the early sixties the NCNW joined forces with women from the YMCA, the National Council of Jewish Women, the National Council of Catholic Women, and Church Women United in order to register voters in Mississippi. This was a dangerous job, and these women faced arrest, threats, and violent opposition for their activities. And while these mainstream organizations challenged the white southern power structure, some rural black women were moved to risk their lives to obtain the right to vote.

For African Americans in the South of the 1960s, registering to vote was not a straightforward task of simply filling out a form at the county clerk's office and receiving a voter registration card. Since the late nineteenth century, southern legislators had passed a host of complicated laws designed solely to prevent blacks from exercising their voting rights guaranteed to them by federal law. For example, blacks who tried to register were given ridiculous tests, such as being asked to recite the entire U.S. Constitution. Or they were charged an exorbitant poll tax. And even those who cleared such hurdles might be further harassed, fired from their jobs, arrested on their way to the polls, or even lynched.

This was the situation faced by forty-four-year-old Fannie Lou Hamer, the granddaughter of a slave and the youngest of twenty children. Hamer was a poor sharecropper from Sunflower County,

Fannie Lou Hamer, one of the first black registered voters in Mississippi.

Mississippi, where none of the county's 13,500 black adults were registered to vote. When Hamer and seventeen others went to the county courthouse in Ruleville to register to vote, Hamer was met by an angry mob of white farmers wearing cowboy hats, carrying guns, and holding back vicious dogs.

The clerk told Hamer that she could register only if she could interpret an obscure section of the Mississippi Constitution. Hamer could not do so and was turned away. On the way back home, the bus she was riding on with the other would-be voters was stopped for no reason and the group was jailed. When she returned home, Hamer's landlord told her to stop trying to register or she would be evicted from the home she had been living in for eighteen years. Hamer moved in with friends and relatives and continued her quest. On the third try, she passed the test and was registered to vote.

Black Women in NOW

Although most African American women worked in grassroots civil rights organizations such as the SNCC, several women of color helped found the National Organization for Women. Duchess Harris explains in *Sisters in the Struggle*:

Contrary to popular belief, there were several women of color involved in the creation of the National Organization for Women (NOW). . . . Three black women—attorney Pauli Murray, who also had a leadership role on the PCSW [President's Commission on the Status of Women]; union organizer Aileen Hernandez; and Shirley Chisholm, who later became the first black U.S. Congresswoman—were involved in the founding of NOW. In 1966, NOW emerged out of the third annual conference, held in Washington DC, of the Commission on the Status of Women. During that period white women who were veterans of the civil rights campaigns were being confronted by the demand for Black Power and decided to shift their energies to the struggle for women's rights. Many upper-middle class, educated white women drew an analogy between sexism and racism, and the founders of NOW declared that they wanted to form "an NAACP [National Association for the Advancement of Colored People] for women."

Pauli Murray was asked to be a founding member of NOW by Betty Friedan after . . . Murray's statements delivered at the 1965 meeting of the National Council of Women. At the council meeting Murray had declared, "If it becomes necessary to march on Washington to assure equal job opportunities for all, I hope I will not back down from the fight." Also in 1965, Pauli Murray published an important article in the *George Washington University Law Review* in which she pointed out that while the brutality that African Americans have endured was far worse than that which women have faced, this did not obscure the fact that the rights of both groups were "different phases of the fundamental and invisible issue of human rights."

She joined the SNCC and began traveling across the South helping others register to vote. One night she was arrested in Winona, Mississippi, where she was jailed and severely beaten. Hamer later described the experience:

Three white men came into my room. One was a state highway policeman. . . . They said they were going to make me wish I was dead. They made me lay down on my face and they ordered two Negro prisoners to beat me with a blackjack. That was unbearable. The first prisoner beat me until he was exhausted, then the second Negro began to beat me. . . . They beat me until I was hard, 'til I couldn't bend my fingers or get up when they told me to. That's how I got this blood clot in my eye—the sight's nearly gone now. My kidney was injured from the blows they gave me on the back.[60]

Despite this experience, Hamer refused to back down and pressed on as an activist in the civil rights movement. In 1964 she took on the role of political organizer and formed the Mississippi Freedom Democratic Party to promote candidates who were sensitive to race issues. Although the party's candidates were defeated, Hamer's experience while trying to register voters helped push Congress to pass the 1965 Voting Rights Act mandating the right to vote for all blacks in every city, town, and county in the United States.

Women and Black Power

At first, however, the new laws passed by Congress were rarely enforced, and people were becoming impatient for change and increasingly angry. In 1966 SNCC leader Stokely Carmichael was arrested at a civil rights rally in Greenwood, Mississippi. After he was bailed out of jail, Carmichael gave a speech to a large crowd that had gathered around the courthouse. As his voice rose above the crowd, he said, "I ain't going to jail no more. . . . What we gonna start saying now . . . is black power."[61] Suddenly the crowd began chanting "Black power! Black power!" and a new movement was born. According to the SNCC, the black power movement "is a call for black people in this country to unite, to recognize their heritage, to build a sense of community. It is a call for black people to begin to define their own goals, to lead their own organizations, and to support those organizations."[62]

Ruby Doris Smith was in that crowd; when she heard Carmichael's inspiring words, she decided black power was the wave of the future. Soon she brought that belief to her job when she took on the role of executive secretary of the SNCC.

Smith and the many other female members of the organization were able to assume leadership roles within the

Riots in the Inner Cities

❦

Whereas the nonviolent methods of protest advocated by the mainstream civil rights organizations played well to television cameras and white audiences, a large segment of inner-city blacks were angry and frustrated with the lack of progress in their lives. This was aggravated by overwhelmingly white and male police departments that resembled an occupying army in black neighborhoods. These officers were quick to beat or shoot anyone regardless of their guilt or innocence. And many black men were extremely angry over the officially sanctioned violence to which Fannie Lou Hamer and other African American women had been subjected. As Stanley Crouch writes in *The Sixties,* "Men did not allow women and children to be beaten, hosed, [shocked with cattle prods], or blown up [when bombs were thrown inside their] Sunday schools. Nonviolence both as a tactic and philosophy was outvoted."

This attitude was clearly demonstrated on August 11, 1965, when violence exploded for six days throughout the 150-square-block Watts neighborhood in Los Angeles. After police beat a black motorist, entire blocks were burned to the ground by irate mobs. Property damage was estimated at $45 million. A new chant, "Burn, baby, burn," was born as hundreds watched white-owned businesses go up in flames.

The Watts riots were the first in a long series of black uprisings during the sixties. In all, over four hundred major and minor riots were recorded in the United States between 1965 and 1969. Although the riots were mainly instigated by males, the aftermath seriously affected mothers with children. An unnamed woman in Detroit, quoted by David Farber in *The Great Age of Dreams: America in the 1960s,* said, "I don't see where the riot accomplished nothing myself but a lot of burnt-up buildings. . . . People couldn't buy a loaf of bread or a quart of milk nowhere in the neighborhood after those riots."

Workers clean up debris after the 1965 Watts riots.

organization, despite appearances that the SNCC was run by men. As SNCC member Joyce Ladner writes,

> None of these [SNCC] women knew they were oppressed because of their gender. No one had ever told them that. They had grown up in a culture where they had the opportunity to use all of their skills and all of their talents to fight racial and class oppression—more radically than anything else. They took their sexuality for granted, for it was not as problematic to them as their race and their poverty.[63]

Despite their positions as strong SNCC leaders, women continued to struggle with gender issues in the black power movement. Many male leaders believed that black men had been kept down for so long by white society that they should be able to become strong leaders without competition from women. Some even feared that women were trying to take over the black power movement, as SNCC leader Angela Davis wrote about her experience in Los Angeles in 1968:

> I ran headlong into a situation which was to become a constant problem in my political life. I was criticized very heavily, especially by male members . . . for doing a "man's job." Women should not play leadership roles, they insisted. A woman has to "inspire" her man and educate his children. . . . Some of the brothers came around only for staff meetings . . . and whenever we women were involved in something important, they began to talk about "women taking over the organization." . . . All the myths about black women surfaced. [We] were too domineering; we were trying to control everything, including the men—which meant by extension that we wanted to rob them of their manhood. By playing such a leadership role in the organization, some of them insisted, we were aiding and abetting the [white] enemy, who wanted to see black men weak and unable to hold their own.[64]

Black Panther Sisters

Davis soon left the SNCC for a new organization called the Black Panther Party (BPP), which proved to be an even more macho and sexist group.

The Black Panther Party was founded in 1966 in Oakland, California, by Huey Newton and Bobby Seale. The goal of the organization was to sign up angry, alienated black males and teach them armed self-defense against the hostile inner-city police forces. Law enforcement officials, obviously, did not appreciate this situation, and almost from the beginning Black Panthers found themselves in a series of violent confrontations with the law. But they had more on their agenda than violence. The Panthers instituted programs that were extremely helpful to single mothers and inspired many women to join the organization. According to the article "A Brief History of the Black Panther Party and Its Place in the Black Liberation Movement," written by Sundiata Acoli,

> [The Black Panther Party] organized community programs ranging from free breakfast for children, to free health clinics, to rent strikes resulting in tenant ownership of their buildings, to Liberation School for gradeschoolers, to free clothing drives, to campaigns for community control of schools, community control of police, and campaigns to stop drugs, crime, and police murder and brutality in the various Black [neighborhoods] across America.[65]

By performing such community-oriented tasks, the BPP became quite popular; by 1969 Black Panther chapters were organized in thirty-seven cities. But the founding members of the BPP had strong male chauvinist tendencies. This was seen in one of the rules of the Black Panther Party, which said, "Sisters did not challenge Brothers [but] stood behind

Author and political activist for SNCC and the Black Panther Party, Angela Davis fought for civil rights.

their black men, supported their men, and respected them."[66]

Elaine Brown was one woman who was, at first, an enthusiastic member of the Black Panther Party. During the late sixties she proclaimed in a BPP newspaper, "We will kill—anyone who stands in the way of our freedom."[67] But Brown quickly became disillusioned with her role within the organization: She was expected to be subservient, clean up after the men, keep her opinions to herself, and give birth to as many children as possible to help swell the numbers of Panthers for the revolution. As Brown states,

[A woman] was considered, at best, irrelevant. A woman asserting herself was a pariah. A woman attempting the role of leadership was . . . making an alliance with the counter-revolutionary, man-hating, lesbian, feminist white [women]. If a black woman assumed a role of leadership, she was said to be eroding black manhood, to be hindering the progress of the black race. She was an enemy of the black people.[68]

Like Brown, some of the women within the BPP realized that they could not function within a blatantly chauvinistic organization. Other women, such as Assata Shakur, simply adapted a more aggressive persona, saying, "[A] lot of us [women] adopted that kind of macho . . . style in order to survive the Black Panther Party. . . . You had to develop this whole arrogant kind of macho style in order to be heard. . . . We were just involved in those day to day battles for respect in the Black Panther Party."[69]

Whatever the survival styles of its female members, the BPP was a short-lived experiment. The radical rhetoric of the party was seen as a challenge to law enforcement officials. During the late sixties federal authorities arrested, wounded, or killed dozens of Black Panthers, and more than four hundred were indicted on various crimes. By the early 1970s the organization had nearly faded from sight.

The Black Panthers were but one small branch of the powerful sixties civil rights movement that permanently changed the status of African Americans during a ten-year period. With women on the front lines of sit-ins, voter registration drives, civil rights marches, and countless other activities, the national mood was galvanized to improve the situation for black Americans. Although much work remained, by 1970 the nation could never return to the bad old days of official segregation and widespread racial violence. And African American women played a leading role in this positive change.

Chapter 4:
Women Protesters

❧

Between March and December 1965, over two hundred thousand U.S. Marine and Army troops landed in South Vietnam, the first large-scale deployment of U.S. forces ordered by President Lyndon B. Johnson to fight the Communist North Vietnamese. For the next decade the United States was mired in the costly and bloody Vietnam War, a divisive conflict that galvanized protest and political activism across the country. Antiwar demonstrations erupted on college campuses almost immediately. Within months, male and female college students organized the first nationwide protest, which took place in the fall of 1965 in Washington, D.C. This demonstration attracted about twenty thousand people, with women at the forefront, many pushing babies in strollers. As the war escalated, so too, did the number of protesters. By the late sixties national demonstrations were attracting more than 250,000 people. And many of these protests turned into violent confrontations as both women and men were teargassed, brutally beaten, and arrested by law enforce-

ment authorities. In fact, female demonstrators were often singled out by police officers for harsher treatment in order to prod male protesters into fighting back to protect "their women."

Women Strike for Peace

Although students led many of the demonstrations, women of every age group and from every walk of life were involved in the antiwar protests. In fact, it was women who staged the first sixties protest against U.S. military policies—four years before the start of the Vietnam War.

Women Strike for Peace (WSP) was founded in 1961 by Dagmar Saerchinger Wilson, a forty-five-year-old Washington, D.C., mother of three who worked as an illustrator for children's books. She was motivated to form the group after the Soviet Union tested a hydrogen bomb (H-bomb) and the subsequent radioactive cloud passed over the United States. Both the United States and the Soviet Union had been exploding H-bombs and contaminating the earth's air and water since the 1950s, and radioactive isotopes had been detected in the breast milk of women around the world. This threat to children prompted more than fifty thousand women in sixty cities to join WSP. Like the women's liberation organizations later in the decade, the group recruited members mainly by word of mouth.

Although WSP was loosely organized, had a small budget, and had no office, the organization picked November 1, 1961, as the day to hold its first protest. At that time WSP members planned to "go on strike" by walking out of their kitchens and off their jobs to demonstrate for an end to nuclear testing. Prior to that day, WSP circulated a flyer that read, "Appeal to All Governments to End the Arms Race—Not the Human Race." Beneath the bold headline the flyer stated, "We strike against death, desolation, destruction and on behalf of liberty and life.... Husbands and babysitters take over the home front. Bosses and substitutes take over our jobs!"[70]

Founder of WSP Dagmar Saerchinger Wilson (left) protests nuclear arms testing on November 1, 1963.

As planned, on November 1 thousands of WSP members protested in Los Angeles, New York, and dozens of other American cities. Carrying signs that read, "Save the Children," "[Nuclear] Testing Damages the Unborn," and "Let's Live in Peace Not Pieces,"[71] this was an unparalleled protest against official government policy. As part of its mission, WSP also appealed to mothers who were married to powerful men: The group sent letters to the Soviet premier's wife, Nina Khrushchev, and John F. Kennedy's wife, Jacqueline, asking them to talk to their husbands about signing a nuclear test ban treaty.

WSP was a uniquely female organization, as founding member Amy Swerdlow writes in *Women Strike for Peace:*

> The women's strike for peace was an instant success in that it drew attention to women's profound fear of the dangers posed to health and life by nuclear testing, and at the same time restored women's voice to foreign policy discourse for the first time since the [end of World War II]. The size of the turnout, its national scope, the traditional and respectable . . . image projected by the women astonished government officials as well as the media. Sophia Wyatt, from London, who marched with the Los Angeles women, tried to determine who and what had brought them out. She asked a woman walking beside her what organization she belonged to. Wyatt reported . . . that the Los Angeles woman replied with a laugh, "I don't belong to any organization. I've got a child of ten."[72]

In response to the publicity garnered by the initial strike, the membership rolls of the WSP swelled as women from across the country—and around the world—joined the group. In the aftermath of their huge success, Wilson worked with seventy-five other founding members of WSP to organize the ever-expanding movement.

Wilson was a reluctant leader and objected to large, bureaucratic mainstream peace organizations run by charismatic leaders. Instead, the steering committee simply called on local grassroots WSP chapters to designate the first day of every month as "Women Strike for Peace Day." Each group could visit local politicians, hold rallies, contact the media, and gain attention for the cause in the manner best suited to them and the region where they lived.

Women Who Testify

Although WSP was composed of mothers, housewives, Girl Scout leaders, and members of the PTA, the group was soon accused by politicians and the press of harboring Communist sympathies and helping the Soviet Union, the sworn enemy of the United States. Wilson dismissed this out of hand, pointing out instead the differences in gender roles while stating her reason for starting WSP:

> You know how men are. They talk in abstractions and prestige and technicalities of the [hydrogen] bomb, almost as if it were all a game of chess. Well, it isn't. There are times, it seems to me, when the only thing to do is let out a loud scream. . . . Just women raising a hue and cry against nuclear weapons for all of them to cut it out.[73]

Throughout the 1960s members of WSP protested the nuclear arms race and the Vietnam War by cleverly utilizing their roles as mothers and housewives, as Blanche Linden-Ward and Carol Hurd Green write:

> These women, mostly married mothers ranging from their twenties on up . . . circulated petitions, spoke at PTA meetings, ran study groups, hosted lecturers, distributed leaflets summarizing facts, canvassed neighborhoods, wrote newspaper ads, placed posters on buses, set up tables in shopping centers, and sent numerous letters appealing both to politicians and their wives. A New York group unfurled a block-long petition on a continuous roll of dish toweling. They bombarded Jackie

Kennedy with the appeal, "Children Are Not for Burning." At demonstrations like the annual Easter Peace Walk, begun in 1963, they often carried large paper flowers with their children's and grandchildren's pictures at the center, shopping bags full of peace pamphlets, and balloons—white for peace or black for mourning, inscribed with slogans like "Stop the Bombing." They wore black armbands and veils, pushed baby carriages, and handed out paper doves, Chinese fortune cookies stuffed with peace messages, and information-packed flyers. They organized motorcades with flying banners to jam busy streets.[74]

While gaining support in the press and and among the general public, WSP also gained enemies because it attempted to join forces with Soviet citizens in ending nuclear testing. The Central Intelligence Agency paid housewives one hundred dollars each to attend WSP meetings and report on supposedly suspicious activities. And in 1962 Wilson and eight other women were called before the House Un-American Activities Committee, a powerful anti-Communist committee in Congress that investigated the political affiliations of thousand of Americans. When a congressman charged that WSP had been infiltrated by Communists, retired teacher and WSP member Blanche

The New WSP Way

T he Women Strike for Peace organization was unique in that it was one of the few groups in the early sixties without men in dominant leadership positions. As a result, the roles women traditionally played in society were used to the advantage of the organization, as Amy Swerdlow writes in *Women Strike for Peace:*

What WSP brought to the 1960s peace movement was a new mode of operation, sometimes referred to as "the new WSP way." The WSP way was intentionally simple, pragmatic, nonideological, moralistic, and emotional. It . . . refused to bar any woman, regardless of her past political affiliations, from membership, and reached out to the apolitical woman in a language that was accessible, free of jargon either political, ideological, or scientific. The [woman] to be reached by WSP flyers, posters, pamphlets, and advertisements was always visualized as the neighbor next door, the woman one met in the doctor's office, stood next to at the supermarket checkout counter, or worked with in the PTA or the League of Women Voters. . . . The school car pool organizational chart and class mother's telephone tree were models for a national decision-making and communications network that substituted for a designated leadership core and a paid staff.

WSP members protest outside the United Nations headquarters in New York City.

From its first day the movement tapped a vast reservoir of moral outrage, organizational talent, and playful irreverence for male political culture that gave its pressure tactics, such as lobbying, petitioning, and demonstrating, a joyful and human face. WSP was one of the biggest stories of 1961 in terms of newspaper and television coverage. And in its first two years WSP was able to make an impact on nuclear policy in a way that few citizens' groups had since World War II.

Posner responded: "You don't quite understand the nature of this movement . . . inspired and motivated by mothers' love for children."[75]

As the investigation wore on, WSP members packed the committee room with young mothers wearing gloves and hats and holding crying babies. Whenever a WSP member had finished testifying, women in the audience presented her with flowers and a standing ovation. As this political theater wore on, the media began to ridicule the politicians. As *New York Times* reporter Russell Baker wrote, the congressmen

> spent most of the week looking lonely, badgered, and miserable, less like dashing [Communist-]hunters than like men trapped in a bargain basement on sale day. . . . The . . . luckless politicians watched the procession of gardenias, carnations, and roses with the resigned look of men aware that they were liable to charges of being against housewives, children, and peace.[76]

Despite official harassment, WSP protests did not fall on deaf ears. On July 26, 1963, Kennedy and Khrushchev signed the Partial Nuclear Test Ban Treaty, banning aboveground testing of nuclear weapons. Kennedy even acknowledged that he heard the WSP message and that it had played a part in prompting him to negotiate the treaty. In addition, Kennedy's science adviser, Jerome Weisner, credited WSP and several other peace groups for persuading the president to ban aboveground nuclear testing.

Although nuclear weapons continued to be tested underground, the treaty was widely celebrated by WSP. Following this victory, WSP was one of the first groups to warn against U.S. involvement in Vietnam, and the group strenuously opposed the war throughout the decade. By 1970 group members were concentrating on environmental issues and the many effects that pollution had on children.

Women in the Free Speech Movement

With its largely middle-class, suburban membership, Women Strike for Peace had impeccable credentials to protest government policies. But when a group of liberal college students at the University of California at Berkeley began to fight their administration over free speech issues, the conflict turned violent and set a precedent for student strikes for the rest of the sixties. As with WSP, women played an important part in the student organization called the Free Speech Movement (FSM).

FSM activity began in late 1964 when Berkeley students began using campus facilities to arrange rallies to aid African Americans in their battle for equal rights. These demonstrations were opposed by several major corporations that contributed financially to U.C. Berkeley. In September 1964 school administrators enacted a campus policy that forbade political activities and fund-raising on campus. Over the course of the next several months, a contentious debate over free speech issues led to the creation of the Free Speech Movement, which attracted thousands of male and female student supporters. Led by

Mario Savio, FSM demonstrations culminated on December 2, 1964, when more than fifteen hundred students walked into the administrative offices at Sproul Hall and held a sit-in to protest the ban on political activities. Male and female protesters were soon violently dragged from the building by police officers and arrested.

Several women took on leadership roles in the FSM. One of them, Bettina

Joan Baez (center) participates in the December 2, 1964, Free Speech Movement sit-in outside Sproul Hall.

Aptheker, was a card-carrying member of the American Communist Party. When this was discovered, U.C. Berkeley dean Clark Kerr dramatically claimed that 49 percent of the FSM participants were Communists, though Aptheker was the only one. FSM leaders took advantage of the shock value of having a real Communist in their midst and gave Aptheker the role of featured speaker at rallies. As she recalled in a 1984 speech at the FSM reunion, "The whole Steering Committee, everybody thought it was a terrific idea to throw the warm, live Communist in [Kerr's] face!"[77]

Whatever Aptheker's role, the FSM embraced typical sexist practices of the time. Whereas men held press conferences, chaired meetings, and planned the movement's direction, women within the movement were assigned tasks such as answering telephones, putting together mass mailings, and running copy machines—sometimes all night.

Although Aptheker herself played a more important part in the protests, reporters seemed to have labeled her simply as Mario Savio's girlfriend. As Aptheker, who was not Savio's girlfriend, states,

Carrying a bullhorn, Bettina Aptheker heads an antiwar march against the Vietnam War.

[A] favorite accusation of the right wing press during the Free Speech Movement was that Mario . . . was an innocent, if misguided, youth who had been seduced *[laughter]* by me, the villainess and evil woman, into criminal and seditious acts. It was generally assumed, even in the mainstream press, that Mario and I were lovers. So much so, that when Mario announced his engagement to someone else, *[laughter]* I was bombarded with questions from a dozen reporters. How was I taking the news? Was I upset? *[laughter]* Was I crushed? What *revenge* would I visit upon this sainted fellow? This is really true, this really happened. . . .

[It] was . . . the case, [however,] that there were women who in one way or another found themselves in situations of performing sexual favors for important movement leaders. That's a fact; that happened. It is also a fact that women activists were also more seriously abused, physically and sexually, both by the police, which is to be expected, and also by men within the movement, which is something that is no longer tolerable.[78]

Despite these conditions, most women accepted their subservient role in the FSM. And those who expressed too much independence were looked upon by these women with scorn. Renée Melody quit the FSM one day when she could no longer tolerate the sexist attitudes of the others:

One afternoon . . . [I] decided to kiss 'em all off and go for a ride on [my] Honda [motorscooter]—that was the high point for me. I remember the glares of the women—the slave women—as I walked out the door . . . just to go and have fun. They hated me! They absolutely hated me! They hated me anyway, because I wouldn't cook and wash dishes. I was never good at cooking, I was never good at typing, and I wasn't going to pretend. I didn't have the consciousness yet that this was a feminist issue; I just knew it offended me, and I wasn't going to do it.[79]

Although issues of gender and sexism played a part in the FSM, the movement was a success, and by January 1965 political speech was no longer banned on campus. The sit-in at Sproul Hall was the first of hundreds of student takeovers by men and women at American college campuses. And young women would find themselves the targets of police and soldiers wielding tear gas, rifles, and bullets. But some women who participated in these protests found new roles and gained a new appreciation for their place in the world, as FSM protester Margo Adler recalls:

[The] FSM gave me an experience of a new kind of freedom, not to speak, to act, or to buy, but to claim the power to come together with others in community to transform and to change. And the FSM was also emotionally powerful because it seemed to be a battle to wrest the control of our lives away from the clerks, the files, and the forms that seemed to be increasingly dominating our lives as students—in other words, from the seemingly invulnerable giants of technology and bureaucracy. . . . The Free Speech Movement gave me and many others a sense of personal power and control over our lives.[80]

Women in SDS

Having won the right to free speech at Berkeley in 1965, the FSM was about to disband when the United States went to war in Vietnam. Practically overnight the FSM transformed into the Vietnam Day Committee (VDC) to protest the war. And the VDC often joined forces with the college-based Students for a Democratic Society (SDS), part of the New Left movement that was gaining popularity at the time.

By 1965 SDS was on the cutting edge of the antiwar movement, organizing demonstrations on campuses across the United States. And it was also encouraging independence among college women. Grassroots organizer Jane Adams was one such woman, having joined SDS because "it was so open and freewheeling, was an organization to which people gravitated in order to come to grips with the nature of the late twentieth century and the world we live in without having to stick to old formulas."[81]

Adams took on the role of regional organizer for SDS in the Midwest. She was given a tiny English sports car and boxes of SDS literature, which she strapped onto the luggage rack. After pasting a "Make Love Not War" sticker on the bumper, Adams set out on the road to spread the word of the antiwar movement in Kansas, Iowa, Nebraska, and Missouri. Students at college campuses in the normally staid farmbelt states were eager to hear about SDS, and Adams proved to be a good messenger. As she states, "I boned up about the [Vietnam] war, delivered literature, and organized a lot of conferences on the war. I thought it important that people talk to each other."[82]

But as women in SDS learned, sexist attitudes like those found in mainstream American society were also inbred in the New Left antiwar organizations. One unnamed male antiwar activist gave his opinion of the jobs females were expected to perform within SDS: "Women made peanut butter . . . they waited on tables, cleaned up, [provided sex]. That was their role."[83] A popular slogan at the time seen on posters, lapel buttons, and picket signs, "Girls say YES to boys who say NO to the draft!"[84] reinforced this attitude. As student organizer Wini Breines recalls, "Sexism was a powerful ingredient in the New Left. Women were often afraid to speak up and when they did they were often ignored."[85]

Even Tom Hayden, a founding member of SDS, expected women to fill traditional roles, no matter how elevated their position or status. Proof of this was offered by University of Wisconsin student Margery Tabankin, the first woman president of the National Students Association in 1967. When Hayden

Women in Vietnam

❧

While hundreds of thousands of women protested against the war, an estimated ten thousand American military women were posted in Vietnam during the 1960s. Incredibly, the Defense Department did not categorize soldiers on a basis of gender, so there is no official count, but a small number of women served in the Women's Army Corps, Women Accepted for Voluntary Service, Women in the Air Force, and the Women Marines. Many of these women worked in noncombat divisions concerned with intelligence, air traffic control, photography, cartography (map making), and other specialties. In addition, about fifty thousand women in Vietnam worked for government and private agencies that specialized in teaching, nursing, entertainment, journalism, and missionary work.

The majority of women in Vietnam were nurses who labored under incredibly difficult conditions. Many volunteered in a rush of patriotic duty and soon found themselves in the midst of a brutal war working in filthy field hospitals and facing a daily regimen of seriously wounded soldiers, mangled peasants, and battle-scarred babies and children. To make matters worse, many of these nurses were in the middle of combat zones, where bombs, gunfire, and mortar attacks were common.

When female vets returned to the United States, few Americans wanted to hear about their trials and tribulations after serving in the extremely unpopular war. And some experienced problems similar to those suffered by male veterans, including flashbacks, nightmares, depression, and diseases caused by toxic substances used in chemical weapons.

A nurse cares for a soldier wounded in the Vietnam War.

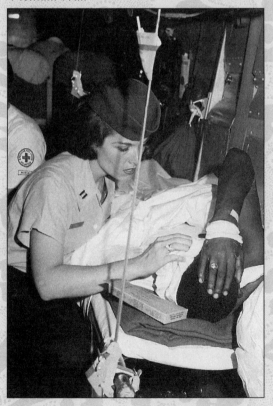

arrived at her university to give a speech against the war, Tabankin says, the first thing he did was hand her a bag of his dirty laundry, telling her to wash it for him by that evening.

Rampant Sexism

Tabankin and other women were forced to come to terms with the fact that SDS was a typical male-dominated organization. Although women constituted five out of nine local chapter delegates in 1964, only one out of seventeen were national council members. No woman held a national office within SDS until 1966, when Helen Garvey was elected assistant national secretary. And it was not until two years later that a woman broke into a top leadership role when Jane Adams became national secretary.

By the second half of the 1960s, women faced violent sexism within SDS. Whenever female members tried to bring up women's issues, they were ridiculed by men and shouted down with catcalls and verbal abuse. In 1966 women demanded that the official SDS political platform include a section on women's liberation; they were bombarded with tomatoes and evicted from the convention.

Many women left the organization around this time, and the exodus intensified after the brutal male reaction to a speech by SDS veteran Marilyn Salzman Webb. In January 1969, at a large SDS rally in Washington, D.C., Webb stood before the crowd and told them that the men were only calling for a revolution to gain power for themselves. Suddenly several male crowd members began to scream obscenities at Webb and shouted for her to take off her clothes. Others screamed that she should be dragged from the podium and raped. Within days, Webb quit SDS and devoted her efforts to women's liberation organizations.

Women Take Over the Campus

Some disenchanted women left the antiwar movement, but others became even more strident in their criticism of the war. By the late sixties, as the war dragged on, protesters realized that although their actions garnered much media attention, they had little affect on government policy. During this time, male and female college students alike began to regularly take over the administration buildings while calling for an end to the war in Vietnam. These sit-ins were often met with overwhelming force by police officers wielding truncheons and tear gas.

On April 23, 1968, more than seven hundred students at Columbia University in New York City took over the Low Library, the administrative offices at Hamilton Hall, and other buildings on campus. The student occupation lasted more than six days and attracted wide coverage from the national and international news media. Although the campus takeover was very serious, the demonstration took on a festive air and even students who were not involved in SDS or other political organizations joined in the protest. Nancy Biberman, one of the protesters who participated in the Columbia takeover, describes the atmosphere at the event: "It was a counterculture event, as well as a political action. There were elaborate feasts in some buildings, socializing, music, dancing. There was a wedding in [the] Fayerwethyer [building] and the two people who were married called themselves Andrea and Richard Fayerwethyer."[86]

The strike lasted for days, during which time students held meetings, talked about issues, read newspaper and magazine stories about the occupation, and drew up long lists of demands, which were debated for hours on end. Biberman describes her idealistic feelings during the occupation:

It's hard to describe, but there was an incredible exhilaration, that here we were making history, changing the world. We had done something that nobody else had done before, and, who knows, maybe we were going to *make the revolution* at Columbia. This was the beginning of the end [for straight America]. Everybody believed that the universe would never be the same, that society would be irrevoca-

On the fourth day of the Columbia University protest of the Vietnam War, students fill the plaza outside Low Memorial Library.

bly changed, that there'd be a revolution in the United States within five years, and a whole new social order. This is really what people believed, and I did, too. It was that kind of heady experience, it really was.[87]

Biberman might have also been inspired by the fact that, by this time, women were no longer letting men dominate the discussion or the chores. According to Friedan, "In the student strike at Columbia in 1968, the girls were supposed to make spaghetti while the men made and carried out the strategies in the occupied buildings—and the girls said no."[88]

After six days, however, more than one thousand New York City policemen moved in to break up the takeover. Finally, at 2:30 A.M., police arrested 722 men and women. They used kicks, punches, and billy clubs on the students, and 148 people were injured, including 20 policemen.

Female Revolutionaries

The feeling that young women and men could permanently change society with protest led to the creation of a radical fringe group known as the Weathermen, whose members believed that the violent overthrow of the government was the only way to bring equality to women and other repressed minorities. With such a philosophy, the Weathermen attracted several notable women, including Diane Oughton, who died when the bomb she was making to blow up a government building accidentally detonated. Although Oughton came from a wealthy family, she had become a radical because she believed that "only in a revolution could men and women be truly equal."[89]

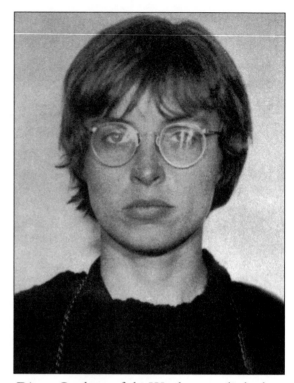

Diana Oughton of the Weathermen died when a bomb she was making exploded.

Susan Stern was another member of the Weathermen who took on a radical, macho role. According to Stern, after she had a "vision of world-wide liberation . . . I ceased to think of Susan Stern as a woman; I saw myself as a revolutionary tool."[90]

Although the Weathermen group only lasted a few years, it garnered great publicity at the end of the sixties but had little lasting effect on the nation. Instead, it was the women who marched, organized, and even typed, made coffee, and ran copy machines who pushed the antiwar movement into national prominence.

To men raised during the 1950s, the concepts of sexism and gender discrimination were simply not issues in the male-dominated antiwar movement until women raised them during the late 1960s. And they came as a shock, as David Lance Goines writes:

[In the] sixties we broke all records . . . jeopardizing our educational futures over the First Amendment and going to jail over the war in Vietnam . . . but when the women who had constituted exactly one-half of the whole shebang turned their eyes to their own inequality and casually mentioned that they wanted a fair shake, we thought they had dropped down from Mars. No kidding. It really came as a surprise.[91]

Although there was initial resistance, many formerly sexist men became feminists themselves in the 1970s, once they understood the issues. And the movement also awakened many women to the sexism prevalent in their midst. Using the backbone of the antiwar movement, women were able to meet each other, organize, and carry on with women's liberation activism long after the Vietnam War ended in 1975.

Chapter 5:
Women in the Counterculture

❦

Millions of women played activist roles in the 1960s, marching for civil rights, peace, and women's liberation. But some women chose to reject all aspects of mainstream society and "drop out" altogether. These women participated in the mass social revolution known as the counterculture movement. Whereas some of these women were politically active, many simply gave up on "the system" that they believed had generated centuries of sexism, racism, poverty, and discrimination. Instead, they became members of the unconventional, nonviolent youth group called hippies. Hippies espoused peace, free love, communal living, rock and roll, back-to-nature politics, and a wide range of mind-altering drugs.

Ground zero for the counterculture revolution was the Haight-Ashbury neighborhood in San Francisco. This section of the city was transformed around 1965, when the powerful hallucinogenic drug LSD, or acid, spilled out of top-secret government laboratories and onto city streets. As thousands of young women

and men began to experiment with the drug, along with marijuana, peyote, and mind-expanding mushrooms, it unleashed a wave of psychedelic intoxication that transformed America almost overnight. A late-sixties study showed that 40 percent of all college students had tried marijuana. Within the counterculture, the figure rose to 90 percent, with 69 percent saying they had tried LSD. In this atmosphere it seemed as if everyone was getting high; even ultraconservative vice president Spiro Agnew's daughter Kim was arrested for possession of pot in 1969.

Led by acid gurus such as Timothy Leary and writer Ken Kesey and San Francisco–based rock bands such as Jefferson Airplane and the Grateful Dead, the socially conservative atmosphere of the early sixties was suddenly fractured by an unprecedented drug-induced revolution against traditional American values. Psychedelic drugs were seen not only as a way to have a good time but also as a path to enlightenment and higher consciousness. And as hundreds of thousands of mostly white, middle-class teenagers followed Leary's famous words and turned on, tuned in, and dropped out, they began to ridicule their parents' world for what they saw as its materialism, blind patriotism, and devotion to mindless hard work.

Young men grew long hair and beards, and women donned either miniskirts or long, flowing peasant dresses, "granny glasses," and love beads. Any and all traditional social institutions were challenged, including marriage, child rearing, and religion. Buddhism, Hinduism, and other Eastern religious practices such as meditation replaced mainstream religion for some. Hundreds of people moved into city and rural communes, where they pooled their money and shared their resources. Fueled by the widespread availability of cheap marijuana and LSD, millions of people bought a ticket into this new world of free love and free thinking.

Author Timothy Leary advocated both the use of LSD and the counterculture movement of the 1960s.

Don't Trust Anyone over Thirty

The counterculture was a movement led by young baby boomers in their teens and early twenties. As youth culture overtook America, *Time* magazine selected for its 1966 "Man of the Year," "the man—and woman—[age] 25 and under."[92]

Meanwhile, a popular sixties slogan, "Don't trust anyone over thirty," was seen on buttons and posters.

These were heady days for young women suddenly liberated from dull suburbia. They could now dress in flamboyant clothing in psychedelic colors and patterns, take drugs, practice carefree sex, and seri-

Defining the Counterculture

Women in the counterculture sought to contrast their lives to what they perceived as "straight" American culture, as Lauri Umansky writes in *Motherhood Reconsidered: Feminism and the Legacies of the Sixties.*

[In the mid-1960s] the symbols of the counterculture began to emerge. For every "plastic" item produced in "Amerika" [as the hippies spelled it], the counterculture offered hand-woven rugs, home-baked bread, bodies awash in their own oils and aromas, freed from chemical tonics and polyester tunics. In contrast to the killing fields of Vietnam and Watts, the counterculture offered the peacefulness of life lived simply, attuned to the dictates of nature. . . . Whereas the separation of humans from nature had produced a repressed, violent, and decadent human species, the reunion of life forms allowed the primal goodness of humanness to emerge. Naked like other animals, the unrepressed human was spontaneous, intuitive, [nurturing], and healthy. Most important, the natural human was "whole," freed from the terrible dictates of a society that demanded the separation of the mind from the body, the body from the spirit, and so on. An ecosystem in miniature, each individual personified holistic purity; together, nature's people would necessarily create harmonious community. . . . The ideal was to eliminate all false boundaries, to create a society of free goods, freely produced, freely distributed. You take what you need, you give what you can. The world is yours to love and work for. No state, no police, no money, no borders, no property. Time and disposition to seek good, seek one another, to take trips deep into the mind, and to feel, to find out what it is to have a body, and to begin to use and make joy with it.

ously antagonize their "straight" parents. But young women taking on the role of hippie flower children were faced with special problems in this "anything-goes" environment. As Timothy Miller explains, in the era before women's liberation, the counterculture was a male-dominated movement:

> Certainly the counterculture was male-defined. . . . Authorship in the underground press was overwhelmingly male. Women were commonly "chicks"; when they were in relationships with men, they were "old ladies." . . . At least at first, the male hippies were as disinclined as males elsewhere in society to allow women equal rights and privileges; the gap between egalitarian hippie rhetoric and male hippie actions may have had some influence on the emerging feminists, many of whom had deep roots in the counterculture.[93]

The hippie movement might have been dominated by men, but the imagery and idealistic philosophies of peace and love had a great appeal to young women. Young women could turn on news programs or pick up *Life* or *Time* magazines and see pictures of carefree "earth mamas" dancing ecstatically in Golden Gate Park, faces painted, wearing flowers in their hair, oblivious to censure or the expectations of others. In *Loose Change: Three Women of the*

Dancing carefree, an "earth mama" celebrates the summer solstice at Golden Gate Park.

Sixties, Sara Davidson describes one such scene at the now-famous 1967 Human Be-In in San Francisco:

> Girls with bare . . . breasts are carrying babies on their backs. Balloons, soap bubbles and hair, hair everywhere! Astrology . . . leather capes, Grateful Dead, [mystical] Sufi dancing, body painting . . . incense and marijuana. Kittens popping out of a

basket. So many funny hats: porkpies, stovepipes. A black man in a loincloth is juggling yellow balls. A toy collie leaps up and catches a ball in his mouth. The crowd slithers and laughs. They are passing around food, crusts of sourdough bread, oranges and jugs of wine. Everyone is photographing everyone else. Flash. Flash. Flash. . . . Mimes in whiteface are bouncing through the crowd. The scariest is a girl with black spider hair and a comb of red feathers like a rooster's on top of her head. Here she comes, look out![94]

Women in Danger

As with most media images, however, the truth of hippie life for women in the Haight was much more complex. As tens of thousands of teenagers streamed into Haight-Ashbury, they began to realize that the reality of life in the neighborhood was quite different from the glossy photos in newsmagazines. The hippie neighborhoods were also attracting rapists, con artists, and dealers of deadly drugs such as heroin and speed (amphetamine). As musician and author Ed Sanders writes, the innocent girls in Haight-Ashbury were like "plump white rabbits surrounded by wounded coyotes."[95]

Thousands of teenage girls ran away from home and flooded into countercul-ture centers such as the Haight, and sexual abuse and other crimes increased rapidly. Whereas some women fell victim to untrustworthy characters, others were protected by strangers. The motorcycle gang Hell's Angels had a mixed record of helping and hurting people, but as Haight-Ashbury resident Cynthia Bowman learned, the bikers could be protective to vulnerable young women. One day Bowman was walking down the street when a man threatened to rape her. As she recalls,

> One of the Angels saw this guy jump on me and he jumped on the guy and threw him onto the roof of a car. . . . And within three minutes there had to be fifty Hell's Angels there, all knocking the [tar] out of this guy. And I was just horrified, crying, terrified—more of the Hell's Angels than the guy. . . . I started trying to get away, walking back to my house, and these Hell's Angels escorted me, pushing their motorcycles to my house, and I remember walking up the steps and all the hippies ran out the back door, thinking the Angels were going to kill us.[96]

Despite such negative experiences, however, many young women found the freedom and creative aspects of counter-culture life exhilarating. By 1970, it is esti-mated that there were almost 5 million hippies in the United States, and nearly half of them were women.

Living on the Streets

With thousands of jobless flower children flocking to hippie neighborhoods, many young women panhandled to survive, often high on drugs, strumming guitars on street corners. Some, such as Bowman, had so little to do that they spent their days simply sitting in front of the Haight-Ashbury home of the psychedelic rock band Jefferson Airplane waiting to catch a glimpse of the famous hippie musicians. As Bowman recalls,

We spent . . . [1968] dropping LSD every other day and sitting across the street from the Airplane mansion, waiting for them to come out. . . . I would just sit there and stare at the big house, as high as I could get, watching them come and go. The only reason I didn't do it every day was because acid only works every other day.[97]

Flower children sit outside a doorway in the Haight-Ashbury hippie mecca of San Francisco.

Women more ambitious than Bowman became artisans, tie-dyeing T-shirts, making beaded jewelry, weaving macramé, or creating some other handicraft work to sell on commission in the "head shops" that lined the streets. Others took on jobs as waitresses, barmaids, temporary workers, and counter help.

With money in short supply, it is little wonder that many women chose to live in crowded hippie "crash pads" where rent was cheap or even free. As celebrated photographer Lisa Law recalls,

Fifteen of us lived together, one room per family, and a kitchen and a communal room. I can't say that I enjoyed that kind of living. It always seemed that women ended up doing a lot more chores than the men. The men played music, smoked the herb, chopped wood and repaired vehicles. The lack of privacy was a test.[98]

And although women did most of the cooking, food was not much to celebrate at most of these early communes. As Bowman recalls, "I would cook the same thing

Outside their "crash pad," fourteen men and women pose for a photo.

Women of the 1960s

every night. Tuna fish, noodles, and cream of mushroom soup."[99]

Women and "Free Love"

Peace and love were the guiding tenets of the hippie movement, but in practice, these virtuous concepts stirred up as much controversy as recreational drug use did. Nudity for example, was an everyday part of life in the counterculture, and hippies were dedicated to breaking the sexual rules imposed on them by their parents. The rallying cries of the day were "Do Your Own Thing," and "Make Love Not War!" As *Newsweek* wrote in 1967,

> For the hippies, sex is not a matter of great debate, because as far as they are concerned the sexual revolution is accomplished. There are no hippies who believe in chastity, or look askance at marital infidelity, or even see marriage itself as a virtue. Physical love is a delight—to be chewed upon as often and freely as a handful of sesame seeds.[100]

Taking part in the sexual revolution meant doing away with notions of monogamy, virginity, and repressed desire. Many women in the counterculture movement, freed from the fear of pregnancy by the birth-control pill, enjoyed and shared carefree sex with much the same appreciation as men. And, perhaps for the first time, sexual pleasure was widely accepted as something that women as well as men could enjoy. As Leah Fritz wrote in one underground newspaper, "As for sex—like eating, like walking in fresh air, like all human activity—it should recreate us, help us to find one another, make us real, and tangible as the earth. It should put us together again, body and soul, male and female, in harmonious intercourse."[101]

Despite these lofty concepts, female flower children were often held to the same standards of beauty as women in the mainstream. Even on communes such as Twin Oaks in rural Virginia, old-fashioned stereotypes remained intact, as Kathleen Kinkade writes in *A Walden Two Experiment*:

> Twin Oaks men, like men elsewhere, found that they preferred women who didn't chase them but just smiled and waited to be approached, that they were turned on by girls who let them do most of the talking, and most of all that it mattered a great deal to them that women have long hair and bodies that somewhat resembled that of a *Playboy* foldout.... [The] closer a girl came to the standard stereotypes of beauty, the more she received the attention of men.[102]

Although this attitude prevailed, members of the counterculture felt that they were part of a large community of like-minded "sisters and brothers" and that sharing everything, from food to drugs to

Free Love and Marriage

✤

In the early sixties, American families were remarkably stable. Many states enforced strict antidivorce laws, making it difficult for most couples to separate, and the divorce rate was only about 10 percent, compared with over 50 percent during the 1990s.

During the later years of the decade, however, the antiwar movement, widespread drug use, and sweeping social changes introduced by the counterculture began to affect even the typical suburban housewife. Some women, tired of housework and suburban conformity, began careers or even "dropped out" to join peace groups or spend time in hippie neighborhoods in big cities. And with the sexual revolution in full swing, the divorce rate more than doubled to 25 percent between 1965 and 1970. Sociologists studying such figures, however, blamed the rise in divorce on men. As Blanche Linden-Ward and Carol Hurd Green write in *American Women in the 1960s: Changing the Future,*

Many argued that the so-called "sexual revolution" [portrayed] women as sex objects as never before and glorified . . . youth, [penetrating] even middle-class, suburban America. It enticed middle-aged men . . . [in the midst of their] "mid-life crisis," to seek younger women in extramarital affairs, in the process breaking up longtime marriages.

love, was not only acceptable but necessary.

Women in Country Communes

By the late sixties the hippie dream had turned sour in some urban neighborhoods as undercover narcotics officers, thieves, dealers, prostitutes, panhandlers, and drug burnouts began to outnumber flower children. At this time, there was a massive exodus of mostly older hippies, especially couples with children. Some headed up to the country in groups to form small rural societies known as communes, where the property was shared by everybody and all members shared work and income.

By the end of the 1960s more than two thousand communes were scattered across the United States, and perhaps a hundred thousand people were living on some sort of commune, each having an estimated twenty to fifty people. Many commune members, however, had grown up in middle-class suburbia and were unfamiliar with the backbreaking work of farming with primitive tools and equipment. Tilling the soil, planting, weeding, cutting wood for heat, building outhouses and other buildings, maintaining automobiles, and caring for livestock proved to be a great strain. And women were still generally assigned the traditional tasks of sewing, cooking, cleaning, and child care. In fact, on some communes women inadvertently assumed the roles of rural farm wives. Kit Leder, who lived on a twelve-member commune in 1969, addresses this issue:

> Even though there was no society-dictated division of labor, even though we had complete freedom to determine the division of labor for ourselves, a well-known pattern emerged immediately. Women did most of the cooking, all of the cleaning up, and, of course, the washing. They also worked in the fields all day—so that after the farm work was finished, the men could be found sitting around talking and taking naps while the women prepared supper. In addition to that, one of the women remained in camp every day in order to cook lunch—it

A hippie woman living on a commune in rural California milks a goat.

was always a woman who did this, never a man. Of course, the women were excused from some of the tasks; for example, none of us ever drove a tractor. That was considered too complicated for a woman. [103]

Commune life, however, was conducive to working out problems, and it was common to hold group meetings nearly every day about topics ranging from buying a new truck to what to cook for dinner. At Twin Oaks, women who were unhappy with their roles at the commune sat down and talked about the subject. Kinkade writes that sometimes women were just as much at fault as men:

[There] is a great deal we can do about the roles men and women are expected to play. We had meetings on the subject and discussed the problem. Was it true that men did most of the talking at meetings? It was. Was this because the group did not respect women? We thought not. The dismal fact was that many of the women did not know as much as the men, had not thought as much, and therefore did not have as much to say. The remedy, then, was with the women themselves. They began to read more, talk more about Community policy, and then speak up at meetings. In a matter of a few months we had a heavy liberation norm going that

drew newcomers into it as soon as they got here. [104]

On communes where women recognized their own power, stereotypical gender roles fell away. As one commune member stated, "All males are chauvinists when they first come here . . . but in a week or two they learn better." [105] In general, men were easily persuaded to cook and clean while women eagerly chopped firewood and drove tractors.

Communal Relationships

Successful communes not only did away with traditional gender roles but also invented new types of families and non-monogamous relationships. With groups of ten to fifty people sharing a common goal, tolerance and compromise were primary values, and members were bound to treat each other as sisters and brothers.

With so many young women and men living together, however, obvious sexual dynamics had to be worked out, along with jealousy and hurt feelings. Kinkade gives an example of a woman who could not choose between two men at the commune:

Jealousy, of course, is a problem. . . . We have not solved this problem. We have, however, taken steps to ease it. Sometimes we succeed and sometimes we don't, but for what it's worth, here is what Twin Oaks cou-

Hippie Communes

In *Sixties People,* Jane and Michael Stern describe, somewhat cynically, the mindset of the women and men who moved to communes in the late 1960s:

The goal of those who split were these: to groove on nature; to grow their own grass [marijuana]; to bake their own bread; to seize cosmic truth by getting *real,* slopping hogs, planting beans, and throwing clay pots. The more primitive, the better.

The main thing country hippies sought was innocence. Hippie logic presumed that innocence was good. From the beginning, acid trips were marketed as a greater way to sweep your mind clean in order to rediscover the glory of being simple. . . .

Although virtually all of them were Caucasian, hippies relished their romantic self-image as nouveau [Native Americans], living in harmony with the universe, fighting against the white man's perverted society of pollution, war, and greed. Country paradise, hippie style, was like a version of Indian life from some old Hollywood movie, in which the long-haired tribesmen in buckskin fringe sit around their tepees smoking pipes, beating tom-toms, and speaking in [self-important] homilies, while the [women] . . . tend the babies and make dinner in elegantly primitive huts.

ples have come up with to help the tensions caused by either multiple relations or changing ones.

One technique is simple scheduling. If a woman cares a lot about two different men, and the men don't like each other, it may be possible for her to agree to spend one day with one, the next with the other. This has been tried various times at Twin Oaks, and it always breaks down after a short time, but it helps to ease the interim. The reason it breaks down is usually that the person in the middle really does prefer one partner to the other and shows it. This leads to withdrawal by the less-preferred partner out of hurt pride. What has been more successful is for the three to spend a lot of time together as a trio. Thus the people who would otherwise be rivals are able to learn to appreciate each other and to gauge the depth of the affair all around.[106]

Despite sensational media reports, few communes experimented with free love, orgies, and sexual anarchy. Instead, most were populated with couples who practiced monogamy for long or short periods of time. As Kinkade writes, "As for orgies, I don't think there are any [at Twin Oaks]. . . . Sex is very important to us, but at the same time we don't make a big deal of it. It is part of our daily lives, but we rarely discuss it. Like eating and working and going for a walk and playing the guitar, it is a part of the good life."[107]

Birthing at the Commune

Instead of wild sexual experimentation, communes offered hippie women secure places to have babies and raise children in a "natural" environment. And giving birth on a commune was often a group celebration. In *Wild Child: Girlhoods in the Counterculture,* Zoë Eakle tells the story of her birth on a Pacific Northwest commune:

> There were about fifty people there on the night I was born. There was plenty of home-brewed liquor on hand, undoubtedly there was music, a guitar or two and maybe even a banjo . . . and lots of potato salad. To this day everyone mentions the potato salad. Those homegrown potatoes are hard to beat. . . . My dad delivered me. My grandmother [who had traveled to the commune from her suburban home] coached him. . . . All of us survived.[108]

Women in communes found that rearing children in such an environment offered many benefits, especially for single mothers. These women could raise babies among dozens of helping hands— and without the burden most single mothers experience of having to take a job outside the home. And instead of sitting in front of a television all day, commune children were often exposed to gentle adults, clean country living in a pastoral setting, and the responsibility and fun of caring for dogs, cats, chickens, goats, and other farm animals. In addition, single mothers often found a good selection of single men at communes to love and help raise their children.

Married couples found similar benefits to rearing children on communes, and thousands of children grew up this way during the late sixties and early seventies. As Eakle writes about her experience, "Growing up [there] was in many ways grand. There were no locked doors and I had the whole forest, beach, and ocean for a playground. There is a glimmer of peace inside me that comes from growing in that place."[109]

Of course, not all aspects of communal life were positive. Young children at communes were often exposed to drugs, some commune members were unsavory characters on the run from the law, education could be haphazard, and there were a few reported cases of child abuse. But in general, children raised at communes learned how to work with others and become self-sufficient at an early age. As one unnamed commune mother commented about her children, "The kids turned out to be bright, creative, interesting and full of life."[110] And in later years, women who lived on communes in the sixties remember those idealistic times fondly. As Joyce Gardner wrote about her experience at Cold Mountain Farm in New York,

We all worked and lived together without any power or authority structure, simply following our own consciousness of what should be done each day.... Children are cared for communally, with the men also caring for them, without any stigma about child-rearing being effeminate. ... And nudity, bodies of all shapes, so readily accepted just as a part of nature. And no power! Only a natural hierarchy of skill, experience, and knowledge.[111]

Bottle-feeding a goat on a commune, children tend to their daily responsibilities.

"Life Was Free"

The vast majority of women who joined the counterculture survived, and even thrived, contributing to dozens of philosophies and cultural practices taken for granted today, including environmentalism, vegetarianism, massage, and Eastern meditation.

In the end, women who lived through the sixties, whether in the city or on country communes, were shaped by the idealism of the times, as Davidson writes:

> In that time, that decade which belonged to the young, we had thought life was free and would never run out. There were good people and bad people and we could tell them apart by a look or by words spoken in code. We were certain we belonged to a generation that was special. We did not need or care about history because we had sprung from nowhere. We said what we thought and demanded what was right and there was no opposition. Tear gas and bullets, but no authentic moral opposition because what could that be? *When you're older you'll see things differently?* We had glimpsed a new world where nothing would be the same and we had packed our bags.[112]

Chapter 6:
Women in Music and the Arts

W omen had to fight to be heard in the civil rights, antiwar, and counterculture movements. But ironically, the voices of women were among the most widely recognized symbols of several groundbreaking sixties events. At the 1964 civil rights March on Washington, gospel singer Mahalia Jackson brought a hush to the huge crowd when she sang the traditional spiritual, "I Been 'Buked [Rebuked] and I Been Scorned" before Martin Luther King's "I Have a Dream" speech. Folksinger Joan Baez also appeared that day, and several months later she attended two major Free Speech Movement rallies at Berkeley, where her protest songs galvanized the resolve of the protesters. And although Crosby, Stills, and Nash had a number-one hit with the widely played "Woodstock," it was Joni Mitchell who wrote the song that immortalized the three-day 1969 concert widely considered the symbol of 1960s music. In music, women in the 1960s were among the vanguard.

Girl Groups

Although "Woodstock" captured the mood of the counterculture generation at the end of the tumultuous sixties, the decade began on an entirely different musical note.

In the early years of the sixties, record companies promoted a genre of popular music aimed straight at the hearts of teenage girls. These songs were recorded by packaged "girl groups" such as the Shirelles, the Crystals, the Shangri-Las, the Ronettes, and the Chiffons. These young singers—most of them in their teens—produced an exhilarating mix of pop, gospel-inspired doo-wop harmonies, and rhythm and blues. They sang with a bold mix of humor and rebellious intensity about subjects dear to the hearts of young women of the time—that is, good boys, bad boys, cheap thrills, the search for perfect love, and, increasingly, standing on their own two feet.

These girl groups, with beehive hairdos, thick eye makeup, tight sweaters, and capri pants projected forbidden images that were just a little bit scary—and very

The Crystals, a girl group whose music was aimed at teenage girls, pose for a photo.

titillating—to their largely conservative suburban audience. As Andrew J. Edelstein writes in *The Pop Sixties,* "When all the girls [at high school] . . . were named Debbie or Laurie or Robyn and wore hair bows [and] penny loafers . . . [girl groups] personified forbidden fruit—the bouffant-ed, gum-chewing, leather-jacketed, mesh-stockinged 'bad' girl."[113]

Though girl groups racked up millions in sales with hits such as "Da Doo Ron Ron," "He's a Rebel," "Leader of the Pack," and "Be My Baby," few got rich from their efforts. As was typical in the music industry at the time, stars of both sexes were routinely denied royalties from the records they made. The money instead flowed to producers, songwriters, and record company executives.

Phil Spector, who created such soul acts as the Crystals and the Ronettes, was one such producer. Spector was legendary for plucking teenage girls from obscurity, utilizing their soulful voices for a string of hits, and discarding them after two or three records.

And the role played by the female stars was strictly limited to providing pretty faces and stellar harmonies. As Crystals member Dee Dee Kennibrew recalls, "We were never allowed any say in what we did at all. We were very young . . . but we were teenagers making teenage music, and we would have liked . . . some input. But no way! There was nothing we could do; Phil Spector was our record company, our producer, our everything."[114] And so it was that when Spector requested that the Crystals record the ode to battering "He Hit Me (and It Felt Like a Kiss)," there was little the group could do to resist.

Veronica "Ronnie" Bennett of the wildly popular Ronettes came to better understand Spector's dark side. She was forced to forgo her status as teenage pop star when she married Spector and assumed a purely domestic role. But Ronnie got more than she bargained for after moving into Phil's Los Angeles mansion, whose grounds were patrolled by attack dogs and surrounded by barbed wire. According to Chuck Miller's article "Ronnie Spector: For Every Kiss You Give Me, I'll Give You Three,"

Ronnie became a prisoner in her own mansion, a songbird with golden handcuffs and a platinum muzzle. Performing was out of the question; she was now Veronica Spector, multi-millionaire producer's wife. Whatever Phil thought she wanted, he bought for her—including three [adopted] kids (including making Ronnie wear a pillow under her dress when people came over to the mansion so they would think she was pregnant) and a car (with its own inflatable replica of Phil Spector to ride shotgun in case somebody thought she was driving alone). . . . [She] recounts stories of how she suffered from bouts of mental and emotional abuse at the hands of Phil Spector, and she eventually turned to an open liquor cabinet in the hopes of making the pain stop.[115]

The marriage ended in divorce four years later, but the producer battled Ronnie for royalties on her records well into the 1990s. Ironically, while women singers were professionally mistreated by male producers, many great female songwriters during the early sixties flourished. Carole King, along with her then-husband Gerry Goffin, penned such girl-group classics as the Shirelles' "Will You Still Love Me Tomorrow?" and the Chiffons' "One Fine Day." Ellie Greenwich, with her husband, Jeff Barry, also wrote several classics, including "Leader of the Pack," "Da Doo Ron Ron," and "Chapel of Love."

Respecting the Women of Motown

Entertainment mogul Berry Gordy, the successful record producer and founder of

Motown Records in Detroit, also capitalized on the girl-group phenomenon. Motown had hit after hit with women who sang songs celebrating love, dancing, and summer in the city.

The seventeen-year-old Mary Wells was one of the first Motown hit-makers, scoring number-one hits with "Two Lovers" and "My Guy," which the producers told her to sing "like you're really *hurt*."[116] In *We Gotta Get Out of This Place*, Gerri Hirshey describes the photo of Wells on the album *My Guy* and her appeal to young women: "[Wells] was soul's Mona Lisa. . . . She's smiling broadly beneath a carefully teased bouffant, almond eyes drawn into a near Egyptian slant by twin strokes of eyeliner. Mary was mohair and sequins, vulnerable and tough."[117]

Wells was also independent. She tired of Motown's rigid control over her career and tried to make it on her own at the age of twenty-one. With little experience in the music business, however, she never achieved the same kind of success she had before her nineteenth birthday.

Unlike Wells, the women in the Supremes racked up five consecutive number-one singles, a feat as yet unmatched by any other group. And under the guidance of Gordy and his hit song-writing team, the group sold so many records that it was one of the few sixties groups that could compete with the all-time top-selling Beatles.

Like many other Motown hit-makers, the Supremes—Florence Ballard, Mary Wilson, and Diana Ross—grew up in public housing in Detroit. The group began singing together in their early teens and were good enough to be hired by Gordy fresh out of high school. After their first hit in 1964—"Where Did Our Love Go?"—the Supremes tapped into the teenage

Mary Wells sang two of the first number-one hit songs for Motown Records.

From Motown to Buckingham Palace

Members of the Supremes, Martha and the Vandellas, and other Motown acts grew up in rough Detroit housing projects. But Motown management wanted these women to put their pasts behind them and refine their personalities so they could play the best nightclubs in America, many of which had been strictly off-limits to black people before the civil rights era. To this end, Motown hired Maxine Powell, who owned a finishing and modeling school, to groom Motown artists. Powell describes her work in David P. Szatmary's *Rockin' in Time: A Social History of Rock and Roll:*

> The [girls] were raw. . . . They were from the streets, and like most of us who came out of the [housing] projects, they were a little crude: some were backward, some were arrogant. They had potential, but they were not unlike their friends in the ghetto. I always thought of our artists as diamonds in the rough who needed polishing. We were training them for Buckingham Palace and the White House, so I had my work cut out for me. . . . Many of them had abusive tones of voice, so I had to teach them how to speak in a nonthreatening manner. . . . Many of them slouched, so I had to show them what posture meant. Some were temperamental and moody; I would lecture them about their attitude. . . . As far as makeup, I worked with all of the girls on wigs, nails, and that sort of thing. And on stage technique, I taught them little things like never turning their backs to an audience, never protruding their buttocks onstage, never opening their mouths too wide to sing, how to be well-rounded professionals. . . . We really wanted young blacks to understand that you do not have to look like you came out of the ghetto in order to be somebody other blacks and even whites would respect when you made it big.

female psyche in the United States and Europe with anthems such as "Stop! In the Name of Love," "Baby Love," "You Can't Hurry Love," and "Back in My Arms Again," all songs that dealt with love, dating, and romance. But, according to Blanche Linden-Ward and Carol Hurd Green, the songs had deeper meaning, with "'women-oriented' themes and proto-feminist messages [that] questioned the costs and consequences of the . . . sexual revolution [that was occurring at the same time]."[118]

Whatever the message of the Supremes, no one could possibly doubt the meaning behind Aretha Franklin's 1967 hit

Psychedelic rock goddess Grace Slick sits at the front of a Jefferson Airplane photo.

"Respect." Franklin, known as "Lady Soul," electrified a generation of young people when she clearly spelled out what she wanted—"R-E-S-P-E-C-T"—in her number-one hit. At the time, "Respect" was seen as the first black feminist anthem, giving voice and meaning to a largely disrespected group, although the song's message has also been celebrated by both genders and nearly every race.

Psychedelic Rock Goddess

No one had to tell Grace Slick of Jefferson Airplane that she deserved respect. During the last third of the 1960s Slick was the premier psychedelic rock goddess, whose soaring, swooping vibrato vocals placed her center stage as one of the first women to front a rock-and-roll band.

When Jefferson Airplane released the album *Surrealistic Pillow* in 1967, music fans across the globe were able to hear the San Francisco sound encapsulated in songs such as "Somebody to Love" and "Plastic Fantastic Lover." Slick quickly became a musical spokeswoman for the counterculture generation after scoring a number-one hit with "White Rabbit," a song laden with references to pills, hallucinogenic mushrooms, and druglike dreams based on Lewis Carroll's *Alice in Wonderland.*

Slick was born to play a leading role in the "do-your-own-thing" 1960s. Always a good student, in high school she studied the lives of powerful women such as Egyptian queen Cleopatra, author Gertrude Stein, singer Ella Fitzgerald, painter Georgia O'Keeffe, and Israeli prime minister Golda Meir. In her autobiography, *Somebody to Love?*, Slick writes that since these women had succeeded,

> I figured my field of possibilities was wide open. I assumed that women who lived for the home front—housewives, homemakers, whatever . . . chose to do that; otherwise, they'd be doing something else. I couldn't imagine anybody doing something they didn't want to do. . . . Financial circumstances might have demanded certain unpleasant activities, but if you did decide to specialize in the homemaking arts, I thought it should be because you were fulfilling a dream, not bowing to societal pressure.[119]

Slick certainly did not follow a conventional path, openly known for her LSD use, wearing stage outfits borrowed from the San Francisco Opera House, and having serial affairs with nearly every member of Jefferson Airplane. But although Slick appeared to be the epitome of a superstar,

she was really very insecure, as she writes about her fame: "I'd always thought [this] was a lofty position reserved only for supermodels, movie stars, and great physical beauties. . . . [I felt like I was] the flat-chested, kinky-brown-haired sarcastic bitch . . . breaking down another barrier in Barbie [Doll] Land."[120]

Slick expertly played the role of a tough counterculture radical, tweaking the nose of straight America with her defiant songs about love affairs, recreational drug use, and overthrowing the government. And while living her life as a musician and revolutionary, Slick inspired a generation of young women to express their feelings, no matter how militant, in song.

Janis Sings the Blues

Along with Grace Slick, Texas-born singer Janis Joplin also shook up the establishment with her unique take on singing—and living—the blues. Joplin was strongly influenced by female blues singers such as Bessie Smith, Etta James, Tina Turner, and Odetta before joining the band Big Brother and the Holding Company in 1966. Dressed in feather boas, oversize round sunglasses, tie-dyed velvet pants, and gypsy blouses, Joplin quickly became famous for wailing out such blues masterpieces as "Piece of My Heart" and "Ball and Chain."

Joplin sang with her eyes closed, her face contorted with pain, clutching a microphone in one hand and a bottle of

Southern Comfort whiskey in the other. She shrieked, moaned, cried, screamed, and pounded her feet, lost in a world of her own while singing, "Come on, come on, come on and take it. Take another little piece of my heart now baby."[121] Joplin preferred alcohol to acid, and her music could not exactly be defined as blues. Nor was it psychedelic acid rock—hers was a sound the hard-drinking singer jokingly called "alkydelic."[122]

In the new feminist age, Joplin presented a public picture of towering female energy, a tough, take-no-prisoners kind of woman who could stand up to men and triumph in the game of love. She shocked sixties journalists by obscenely comparing her performances to sex and was widely known for her sexual exploits with both women and men. But Joplin was never a great beauty, and she hid behind the powerful icon of rock superstar to cover her gnawing insecurities. As friend Odetta recalls, "Around her success there was a terrible loneliness that was unbelievable."[123]

Like other rock stars who create an outrageous public image for themselves, Joplin became trapped in the role of a rowdy, drunken blues singer, often known as much for her shocking behavior as for her music. As Alice Echols writes in *Scars of Sweet Paradise,* "Janis's audience did eat up her flamboyant exploits, but it was Janis herself who made her life a spectacle. She seemed to feel that her amazing perform-ances weren't enough, that she had to wear her suffering on her sleeve all the time or her fans would turn away."[124] Joplin never did resolve the differences between her truly vulnerable inner self and her hard-bitten public image. She died of a heroin overdose on October 4, 1970, at the age of twenty-seven, barely four years into a meteoric musical career.

Despite her short and tragic life, Joplin served as a great influence on the female vocalists who followed. The singer has been credited with influencing belters and balladeers from Bette Midler to Sheryl Crow to country singer Faith Hill. And to her female fans, she symbolized rebellion against traditional feminine roles in an era still saturated with stereotypes of femininity. As Echols writes,

> Janis's success had a lot to do with timing: she expressed women's anger and disappointment before feminism legitimized their expression. Her refusal to sound or look pretty prefigured feminism's demolition of good-girl femininity, and much of her music. . . protests women's powerlessness in matters of the heart.[125]

Joni Mitchell's Personal Expression

Whereas Joplin and Slick thrived on shock value, Canadian-born singer-songwriter Joni Mitchell sang intimate songs about life,

Lips puckered and eyes closed, Janis Joplin wails the blues into the microphone.

love, and longing with an irresistible eloquence and grace. Calling her style "sock-it-to-me-softly"[126] music, Mitchell was one of the first popular singers to write both the words and the music to her songs, and her literate lyrics often dealt with the most personal details of her life. She also wrote several songs, such as "Woodstock," that became anthems expressing the thoughts and feelings of a generation. In "Big Yellow Taxi," perhaps the first ode to environmentalism, the singer laments paving paradise to put up a parking lot.

Armed only with her voice, guitar, and piano, Mitchell had a more difficult time getting people's attention during the wild and crazy sixties. As she says, "My music is not designed to grab instantly. It's designed to wear for a lifetime, to hold up like fine cloth."[127] And with such subtlety, Mitchell also had trouble commanding respect and gaining individual identity in the male-dominated music business. She was often compared—both favorably and unfavorably—with legendary rock icon Bob Dylan. Mitchell bristles at the comparison, saying, "Were I a male I think it would have been different. The critics didn't lump Dylan in with others."[128] And when told that one critic called her music "cranky," Mitchell responded angrily at the stereotypical roles that women were expected to play, saying, "Dylan is far crankier than me. . . . Do they call Dylan cranky for making social commentary? It's like an angry man is an angry man and an angry woman is a bitch."[129]

Despite the genius of her music and her widespread success, Mitchell continued to face sexism. As Echols explains, "Mitchell's problem is that she's never been a bad girl. She was never bawdy, tough, or obviously androgynous. Finally, the music for which she is best known reveals a vulnerability at odds with the angry . . . pose [that men could relate to]."[130]

Even the then-leading counterculture journal *Rolling Stone* ran an article proclaiming Mitchell "Old Lady of the Year," complete with a diagram (erroneously) listing all the famous men the singer had had affairs with and which of her songs were about whom. Mitchell was so upset by the article that she refused requests for interviews from the magazine for eight years. During that time critics savaged her albums, which are now considered brilliant classics. Mitchell's influence on singers from Rickie Lee Jones to Sarah McLachlan, Jewel, Paula Cole, the Indigo

Joni Mitchell, one of the first female singers to write her own music and lyrics, strums her guitar.

Girls, Fiona Apple, and many others is undeniable.

Words of Love, Hate, and Madness

Joni Mitchell is revered for the imagery and poetry she so prolifically created in the words to her songs. And in the era when Mitchell began her career, a few women writers were making waves in print as well as in song.

Nonfiction authors such as feminist Betty Friedan and environmentalist Rachel

Carson, author of the pesticide exposé *Silent Spring,* sold millions of books in the sixties while drawing attention to important causes. Southern author Harper Lee did the same with *To Kill a Mockingbird,* a fictional story based on life in a small town in Alabama. Published in 1960, Lee's novel is told from the viewpoint of a young girl nicknamed Scout, who, wise beyond her years, describes the racism and prejudice around her. Although Lee won a Pulitzer Prize for her story in 1961, she never wrote another novel. But before the rise of the "make love not war" movement, Lee

Singer and Activist Joan Baez

Joan Baez played a dual role in the 1960s. Not only was she a best-selling folksinger whose style was imitated by countless earnest young women with guitars, but she was also an outspoken supporter of the civil rights and antiwar movements.

In the early sixties, Baez released several million-selling albums that remained on the pop charts for years. She was the female face of American folk music, profiled in magazines and drawing crowds at concerts and festivals. But having grown up as a woman of Mexican American heritage, the folksinger had often felt the sting of prejudice. After she achieved stardom, she used her popularity to draw attention to the discrimination then rampant in American society. In 1963 she sang at the March on Washington led by Martin Luther King Jr., and her version of "We Shall Overcome" sung that day became an anthem at civil rights and antiwar rallies across the nation.

In 1965 the singer used the proceeds from her successful career to found the Institute for the Study of Non-Violence in Carmel Valley, California. In 1966 Baez jeopardized her career—and her freedom—by refusing to pay income taxes, asserting that 60 percent of tax revenues went to the Defense Department and she, in good conscience, could not support the Vietnam War in any way. The Internal Revenue Service (IRS) warned her that she could go to prison for refusing to pay taxes, but instead the IRS put a lien on Baez's house and car and simply confiscated the cash proceeds from her concerts.

Throughout the sixties Baez continued to put her political beliefs before her musical career. In 1968 she married an unknown student protest leader, David Harris, whom she admired for his principled stand against the war. Harris was soon imprisoned for refusing to serve in the army when drafted, and Baez fought for several years to free him. Her recording career and activism continues today.

proved something of a soothsayer in an article titled "Love—in Other Words," for *Vogue*. In the piece, the author explores the subjects of love, death, and materialism in words that would become much more common in the pronouncements by hippies and Eastern gurus by the end of the decade:

Few of us achieve compassion; to some of us romance is a word; in many of us the ability to feel affection has long since died; but all of us at one time or another—be it for an instant or for our lives—have departed from ourselves: we have loved something or someone. Love, then is a paradox: to have it, we must give it. Love . . . is a direct action of mind and body.

Without love, life is pointless and dangerous. Man is on his way to Venus, but he still hasn't learned to live with his wife. Man has succeeded in increasing his life span, yet he exterminates his brothers six million at a whack. Man now has the power to destroy himself and his planet: depend upon it, he will—should he cease to love.

The most common barriers to love are greed, envy, pride, and four other drives formerly known as sins. There is one more just as dangerous: boredom. The mind that can find little

excitement in life is a dying one; the mind that can not find something in the world that attracts it is dead, and the body housing it might as well be dead, for what are the uses of the five senses to a mind that takes no pleasure in them?[131]

Whereas Lee explored the boundaries of love and hate, Sylvia Plath used poetry to plumb the depths of her personal depression, madness, and suicidal tendencies. Plath was a brilliant poet, but her life was haunted by a difficult marriage to poet Ted Hughes and the death of her father when she was only eight. Her first book of poems, *The Colossus*, was published in 1960 and was not well received. Meanwhile, as her marriage began to dissolve, Plath wrote the semiautobiographical novel *The Bell Jar*, which, according to Linden-Ward and Green, presents "a scathing, personal analysis of the roles and images to which women had to conform."[132]

After completing *The Bell Jar*, Plath wrote dozens of poems that have since cemented her reputation as an important sixties poet. These poems defied stereotypical female roles by using bitter irony and illusion to create feelings of confusion, paranoia, and contempt common to Plath's mental illness.

Plath, who had had attempted suicide several times, succeeded in killing herself in February 1963 at the age of thirty-one.

Seeking mental sanctuary through writing, Sylvia Plath became a renowned novelist and poet of the 1960s.

The Bell Jar was published posthumously and has been recognized as one of the great novels of the 1960s, exploring personal themes of mental illness that had been previously avoided in literary circles.

Chronicling the Real World

During the sixties, it was not only authors who examined the dark side of life in their artistic work. Many women chronicled the political and cultural signs of the times as journalists and photographers. Diane Arbus was a photographer for the prestigious New York fashion industry during the late fifties. But Arbus was dissatisfied with taking pictures of glamorous models and began pointing her camera instead at people living on the outskirts of society. In the early sixties, Arbus took hundreds of photos of prostitutes, transvestites, mental patients, nudists, and sideshow circus acts—people she called freaks. Having grown up in a safe, middle-class environment, Arbus explains why she took on the role as photographic messenger from the fringe:

> Freaks was a thing I photographed a lot . . . and it had a terrific kind of excitement for me. I just used to adore them. I still do adore some of them. I don't quite mean they're my best friends but they made me feel a mixture of shame and awe. There's a quality of legend about freaks. Like a person in a fairy tale who stops you and demands that you answer a riddle. Most people go through life dreading they'll have a traumatic experience. Freaks were born with their trauma. They've already passed their test in life. They're aristocrats.[133]

The stark realism that Arbus captured in her photographs allowed her to thrive in the exclusive New York art scene, far from the seedy nudist camps, freak shows, and transvestite bars patronized by her subjects. Although the photographer received

Photographing the Sixties

❧

Rock and roll dominated the music industry during the 1960s, and male performers and producers dominated rock and roll, but a number of women gained unfettered access to the rock world as photographers. As the "Linda McCartney's Sixties: Portrait of an Era" website demonstrates, some camera-wielding women were as gifted as the stars they were photographing, and a few became celebrities in their own right.

Linda McCartney covered the music scene of the Sixties first as house photographer of New York's Fillmore East concert hall, and then as the first photographer of the budding *Rolling Stone* magazine. Combining photography with her love of rock and roll, Linda specialized in capturing the character of the new British and West Coast bands as they visited New York. In clubs and nightspots, she photographed the likes of The Doors and The Who before they catapulted to stardom. She was there, at recording sessions and rehearsals, back stage, on tour, and in concert, an accepted "band member

whose instrument was the camera," as she once put it.

Her unposed portraits of the greats of the Sixties music scene capture the spirit not only of her subjects but that of the time. Her spontaneous style was the perfect match for the live-for-the-moment decade.

She traveled to Los Angeles and San Francisco and, in 1967, went on assignment to London for the book *Rock and Other Four-Letter Words*. Here her photography . . . caught the eye of Beatles manager Brian Epstein, who invited her to photograph The Beatles at the press launch of their new album *Sgt. Pepper's Lonely Hearts Club Band*. It was there that Linda met Paul McCartney, and two years later, they married. . . .

If Linda's photographs of the Sixties defined a period in time, the Sixties defined Linda as a photographer. She emerged from the Sixties as Linda Eastman McCartney to go on to become one of the most distinguished women photographers of our time.

several prestigious Guggenheim fellowships throughout the sixties, like Plath, she suffered from serious depression and suicidal tendencies. Arbus killed herself in July 1971, but her work has inspired countless photographers to erase the line between camera operator and subject and portray sometimes unattractive subjects with a sympathetic eye.

Women Artists

By projecting sympathy and compassion, Arbus was able to put her subjects at ease in a way that a male photographer might not have been able to accomplish. And in the art world, photography was one of the few pursuits that were open to women. Those who painted or sculpted, however, often faced blatant sexism from the mainstream art establishment. In the early sixties artist Georgia O'Keeffe felt this sting when her paintings of flowers and wildlife—now considered priceless masterpieces—were

Marisol sculpted lifesize statues of her own body, gaining notoriety as a highly talented artist.

reviewed by one critic who said, "All these pictures say is 'I want to have a baby.'"[134]

Younger female artists abandoned the formal art world, populated as it was with wealthy elites, and instead chose to pursue popular, or pop, art that was more expressive of the times. Paris-born Marisol Escobar, known simply as Marisol, created lifesize sculptures based on her own body parts while exhibiting a flair for self-promotion. In an example of the sexism of the day, she was often compared with the most well known pop artist, saying she was the "female Andy Warhol," who himself called Marisol "the first girl artist with glamour."[135]

Eva Hesse, another pop artist, blended painted works with found objects such as rope, metal, rubber, cheesecloth, and wire to create a new form of sculpture that represented the impermanence of life by decaying over time. These works, which could be bent and shaped, were also said to represent Hesse's feminine flexibility—and fragility—in the stodgy male-oriented art world.

Trying to Make a Better World

From the art galleries of New York to the concert halls of San Francisco, women played important roles in music and the arts during the 1960s. Whether providing lilting harmonies in a girl group or exploring the darker sides of sanity, women provided a perspective that was as needed as it was unique. With a keen eye for fairness and social justice, female artists were often forced into the role of outsiders while at the same time providing inspiration and encouragement to millions of young women who themselves wanted to shake up the status quo.

In this way, the spirit of the sixties revolution lives on in the twenty-first century. And there are few young women today who cannot trace the roots of their success, their freedom, and their equality to their mothers, grandmothers, and great-grandmothers who fought the establishment and made the world a better place for both women and men.

Notes

Introduction: A Decade of Profound Social Change

1. Blanche Linden-Ward and Carol Hurd Green, *American Women in the 1960s: Changing the Future*. New York: Twayne, 1993, p. xiv.

Chapter 1: Women in the Mainstream

2. Betty Friedan, *The Feminine Mystique*. New York: Norton, 1963, pp. 15–16.
3. Helena Znaniecka Lopata, *Occupation: Housewife*. New York: Oxford University Press, 1971, p. 183.
4. Sonia Pressman Fuentes, "Sex Maniac," Feminism/Women in Philosophy, 1999. www.erraticimpact.com.
5. Quoted in Friedan, *The Feminine Mystique,* pp. 215–16.
6. Quoted in Linden-Ward and Green, *American Women in the 1960s,* p. xiii.
7. Quoted in Linden-Ward and Green, *American Women in the 1960s,* p. xii.
8. Friedan, *The Feminine Mystique,* p. 19.
9. Helen Gurley Brown, *Sex and the Single Girl*. New York: Bernard Geis Associates, 1962, pp. 5–6.
10. Melissa Hantman, "Helen Gurley Brown," Salon.com, September 26, 2000. http://dir.salon.com.
11. Quoted in Hantman, "Helen Gurley Brown."
12. Hantman, "Helen Gurley Brown."
13. Fuentes, "Sex Maniac."
14. Carol Hymowitz and Michaele Weissman, *A History of Women in America*. New York: Bantam Books, 1978, pp. 315–16.
15. Quoted in Hymowitz and Weissman, *A History of Women in America,* p. 316.
16. Quoted in Linden-Ward and Green, *American Women in the 1960s,* p. 97.
17. Quoted in Bonnie Watkins and Nina Rothchild, *In the Company of Women*. St. Paul: Minnesota Historical Society, 1996, p. 79.
18. June Sochen, *Herstory*. New York: Alfred, 1974, p. 382.
19. Linden-Ward and Green, *American Women in the 1960s,* p. 122.

20. Quoted in Watkins and Rothchild, *In the Company of Women,* p. 241.

Chapter 2: Women Feminists

21. John F. Kennedy, "President's Commission on the Status of Women." http://womenshistory.about.com.
22. Eleanor Roosevelt, "My Day—Women's Issues," American Experience. www.pbs.org.
23. Quoted in Linden-Ward and Green, *American Women in the 1960s,* p. 8.
24. Quoted in Leila J. Rupp and Verta Taylor, *Survival in the Doldrums.* New York: Oxford University Press, 1987, p. 173.
25. Quoted in Watkins and Rothchild, *In the Company of Women,* p. 10.
26. Rupp and Taylor, *Survival in the Doldrums,* p. 176.
27. Fuentes, "Sex Maniac."
28. Quoted in Watkins and Rothchild, *In the Company of Women,* p. 45.
29. Fuentes, "Sex Maniac."
30. Quoted in Hymowitz and Weissman, *A History of Women in America,* p. 345
31. Betty Friedan, *It Changed My Life.* New York: Random House, 1976, p. 107.
32. Friedan, *It Changed My Life,* p. 108.
33. Quoted in Watkins and Rothchild, *In the Company of Women,* pp. 19–20.
34. Quoted in Watkins and Rothchild, *In the Company of Women,* p. 34.
35. Quoted in Watkins and Rothchild, *In the Company of Women,* pp. 274–75.
36. Pat Mainardi, "The Politics of Housework," CWLU Herstory. www.cwluherstory.com.
37. Quoted in Hymowitz and Weissman, *A History of Women in America,* p. 345.
38. Mainardi, "The Politics of Housework."
39. Friedan, *It Changed My Life,* p. 116.
40. Quoted in Hymowitz and Weissman, *A History of Women in America,* pp. 348–49.
41. Sally Kempton, "Cutting Loose," *Esquire,* July 1970.
42. Quoted in Lillian Faderman, *Odd Girls and Twilight Lovers.* New York: Columbia University Press, 1991, p. 188.
43. David Farber, *The Great Age of Dreams: America in the 1960s.* New York: Hill and Wang, 1994, p. 258.

44. Phyllis Chesler, *Women and Madness.* Garden City, NY: Doubleday, 1972, pp. 243–44.

Chapter 3: Women in the Civil Rights Movement

45. Quoted in Bettye Collier-Thomas and V. P. Franklin, eds., *Sisters in the Struggle.* New York: New York University Press, 2001, p. 90.

46. Malcolm X, with Alex Haley, *The Autobiography of Malcolm X.* New York: Ballantine Books, 1990, p. 226.

47. Farber, *The Great Age of Dreams,* p. 11.

48. Farber, *The Great Age of Dreams,* p. 77.

49. Deborah Gray White, *Too Heavy a Load.* New York: Norton, 1999, pp. 179–80.

50. Zita Allen, *Black Women Leaders of the Civil Rights Movement.* New York: Franklin Watts, 1996, p. 72.

51. Quoted in Allen, *Black Women Leaders of the Civil Rights Movement,* pp. 73–74.

52. Quoted in Vicki L. Crawford, Jacqueline Anne Rouse, and Barbara Woods, eds., *Women in the Civil Rights Movement.* Brooklyn, NY: Carlson, 1990, p. 1.

53. Quoted in Allen, *Black Women Leaders of the Civil Rights Movement,* p. 69.

54. Quoted in Crawford, Rouse, and Woods, *Women in the Civil Rights Movement,* pp. 2–3.

55. Quoted in Allen, *Black Women Leaders of the Civil Rights Movement,* p. 82.

56. Quoted in White, *Too Heavy a Load,* p. 178.

57. Quoted in Collier-Thomas and Franklin, *Sisters in the Struggle,* p. 86.

58. Quoted in Collier-Thomas and Franklin, *Sisters in the Struggle,* p. 89.

59. Quoted in Collier-Thomas and Franklin, *Sisters in the Struggle,* p. 91.

60. Quoted in "Fannie Lou Hamer, 1917–1977," 1997. www.beejae.com.

61. Quoted in Collier-Thomas and Franklin, *Sisters in the Struggle,* p. 198.

62. Quoted in Collier-Thomas and Franklin, *Sisters in the Struggle,* p. 198.

63. Quoted in Collier-Thomas and Franklin, *Sisters in the Struggle,* p. 204.

64. Quoted in Collier-Thomas and Franklin, *Sisters in the Struggle,* p. 208.

65. Sundiata Acoli, "A Brief History of the Black Panther Party and Its Place in the Black Liberation

Movement," April 2, 1985. www.cs. oberlin.edu.

66. Quoted in White, *Too Heavy a Load,* p. 220.

67. Quoted in Linden-Ward and Green, *American Women in the 1960s,* p. 63.

68. Quoted in White, *Too Heavy a Load,* p. 220.

69. Quoted in Collier-Thomas and Franklin, *Sisters in the Struggle,* p. 243.

Chapter 4: Women Protesters

70. Quoted in Amy Swerdlow, *Women Strike for Peace.* Chicago: University of Chicago Press, 1993, p. 18.

71. Quoted in Swerdlow, *Women Strike for Peace,* p. 15.

72. Quoted in Swerdlow, *Women Strike for Peace,* p. 16.

73. Quoted in Swerdlow, *Women Strike for Peace,* p. 15.

74. Linden-Ward and Green, *American Women in the 1960s,* p. 164.

75. Quoted in Linden-Ward and Green, *American Women in the 1960s,* p. 165.

76. Quoted in Linden-Ward and Green, *American Women in the 1960s,* pp. 165–66.

77. Bettina Aptheker, "Women and the FSM," March 20, 2002. www.straw.com.

78. Aptheker, "Women and the FSM."

79. Quoted in David Lance Goines, *The Free Speech Movement: Coming of Age in the 1960s.* Berkeley, CA: Ten Speed, 1993, p. 476.

80. Margo Adler, "Heretic's Heart: A Journey Through Spirit and Revolution," 1997. www.straw.com.

81. Quoted in Ronald Chepesiuk, *Sixties Radicals, Then and Now: Candid Conversations with Those Who Shaped the Era.* Jefferson, NC: McFarland, 1995, p. 56.

82. Quoted in Chepesiuk, *Sixties Radicals,* p. 65.

83. Quoted in Susan Dworkin, *She's Nobody's Baby: A History of American Women in the Twentieth Century.* New York: Simon & Schuster, 1983, p. 162.

84. Quoted in Goines, *The Free Speech Movement,* p. 475.

85. Quoted in Linden-Ward and Green, *American Women in the 1960s,* p. 159.

86. Quoted in Joan Morrison and Robert K. Morrison, eds., *From Camelot to Kent State: The Sixties Experience in the Words of Those Who Lived It.* New York: Times Books, 1987, pp. 271–72.

87. Quoted in Morrison and Morrison, *From Camelot to Kent State,* p. 273.

88. Friedan, *It Changed My Life,* p. 108.

89. Quoted in Linden-Ward and Green, *American Women in the 1960s,* p. 160.

90. Quoted in Linden-Ward and Green, *American Women in the 1960s,* p. 160.

91. Goines, *The Free Speech Movement,* p. 478.

Chapter 5: Women in the Counterculture

92. Quoted in Sara Davidson, *Loose Change: Three Women of the Sixties.* Garden City, NY: Doubleday, 1977, p. 100.

93. Timothy Miller, *The Hippies and American Values.* Knoxville: University of Tennessee Press, 1991, p. 16.

94. Davidson, *Loose Change,* p. 107.

95. Quoted in Alice Echols, *Shaky Ground: The Sixties and Its Aftershocks.* New York: Columbia University Press, 2002, p. 45.

96. Quoted in Michael Gross, *My Generation.* New York: HarperCollins, 2000, p. 92.

97. Quoted in Gross, *My Generation,* p. 92.

98. Lisa Law, "Summer of Love Photos," 1999. www.summerof love.org.

99. Quoted in Gross, *My Generation,* p. 92.

100. Quoted in Linden-Ward and Green, *American Women in the 1960s,* p. 252.

101. Quoted in Miller, *The Hippies and American Values,* p. 54.

102. Kathleen Kinkade, *A Walden Two Experiment.* New York: William Morrow, 1973, p. 170.

103. Quoted in Miller, *The Hippies and American Values,* p. 96.

104. Kinkade, *A Walden Two Experiment,* p. 170.

105. Quoted in Kinkade, *A Walden Two Experiment,* p. 171.

106. Kinkade, *A Walden Two Experiment,* p. 167.

107. Kinkade, *A Walden Two Experiment,* p. 171.

108. Quoted in Chelsea Cain, ed., *Wild Child: Girlhoods in the Counterculture.* Seattle: Seal, 1999, p. 8.

109. Quoted in Cain, *Wild Child,* p. 9.

110. Quoted in Timothy Miller, *The Sixties Communes.* Syracuse, NY: Syracuse University Press, 1999, p. 239.

111. Quoted in Miller, *The Sixties Communes,* p. 235.

112. Davidson, *Loose Change,* p. 3.

Chapter 6: Women in Music and the Arts

113. Andrew J. Edelstein, *The Pop Sixties.* New York: World Almanac, 1985, p. 11.

114. Quoted in Linden-Ward and Green, *American Women in the 1960s*, p. 231.

115. Chuck Miller, "Ronnie Spector: For Every Kiss You Give Me, I'll Give You Three." http://home town.aol.com.

116. Quoted in Gerri Hirshey, *We Gotta Get Out of This Place*. New York: Atlantic Monthly, 2001, p. 63.

117. Hirshey, *We Gotta Get Out of This Place,* p. 63.

118. Linden-Ward and Green, *American Women in the 1960s,* p. 236.

119. Grace Slick, *Somebody to Love?* New York: Warner Books, 1998, p. 7.

120. Slick, *Somebody to Love?* p. 104.

121. Quoted in Linden-Ward and Green, *American Women in the 1960s,* p. 247.

122. Quoted in Jim DeRogatis, *Kaleidoscope Eyes.* New York: Citadel, 1996, p. 57.

123. Quoted in Alice Echols, *Scars of Sweet Paradise.* New York: Metropolitan Books, 1999, p. 276.

124. Echols, *Scars of Sweet Paradise,* p. 278.

125. Echols, *Scars of Sweet Paradise,* p. 306.

126. Quoted in Linden-Ward and Green, *American Women in the 1960s,* p. 243.

127. Quoted in Echols, *Shaky Ground,* p. 208.

128. Quoted in Echols, *Shaky Ground,* p. 221.

129. Quoted in Echols, *Shaky Ground,* p. 221.

130. Echols, *Shaky Ground,* p. 221.

131. Harper Lee, "Love—in Other Words," *Vogue,* April 15, 1961, p. 64.

132. Linden-Ward and Green, *American Women in the 1960s,* p. 316.

133. Quoted in Sara Ironman, "Diane Arbus." www.temple.edu.

134. Quoted in Linden-Ward and Green, *American Women in the 1960s,* p. 261.

135. Quoted in Linden-Ward and Green, *American Women in the 1960s,* p. 264.

For Further Reading

Berkeley Arts Center Association, *The Whole World Is Watching.* Berkeley, CA: Berkeley Arts Center Association, 2001. A book of photographs portraying various aspects of the 1960s and 1970s peace and justice movements with essays by various eyewitnesses to the events. The book accompanies a 2001 exhibition of photographs at the Berkeley Arts Center.

Chelsea Cain, ed., *Wild Child: Girlhoods in the Counterculture.* Seattle: Seal, 1999. Fourteen essays by young women detailing their lives while growing up with hippie parents during the 1960s and 1970s.

Andrew J. Edelstein, *The Pop Sixties.* New York: World Almanac, 1985. A witty and irreverent look at the cultural icons of the sixties, including fashion, music, television, film, and cars.

Editors of Time-Life Books, *Turbulent Years: The Sixties.* Alexandria, VA: Time-Life Books, 1998. A big, colorful volume that covers all aspects of 1960s culture, including the war in Vietnam, assassinations, hippies, communes, rock and roll, and the antiwar movement.

Lynda Rosen Obst, ed., *The Sixties.* New York: Rolling Stone, 1977. A book about the 1960s in the words of some famous people who lived through the decade. A year-by-year summary of famous events is included, and the oversize book is interspersed with full-page black-and-white photos of famous events both happy and tragic.

Jane Stern and Michael Stern, *Sixties People.* New York: Alfred A. Knopf, 1990. An entertaining book with chapters describing the music, fashion, and culture of surfers, folksingers, hippies, rebels, "Mr. and Mrs. Average," and other characters of the sixties along with many pages of photos, album art, and so on.

Works Consulted

Books

Zita Allen, *Black Women Leaders of the Civil Rights Movement*. New York: Franklin Watts, 1996. This book provides biographies of women who led the fight for black rights throughout the twentieth century.

Patricia Bosworth, *Diane Arbus*. New York: Knopf, 1984: The biography of a photographic genius whose haunting pictures of circus freaks and other social pariahs became hallmarks of sixties art.

Helen Gurley Brown, *Sex and the Single Girl*. New York: Bernard Geis Associates, 1962. The manifesto for the single sixties "perky" girl with tips on food, fashion, dating, romance, and catching a man.

Rachel Carson, *Silent Spring*. Boston: Houghton Mifflin, 1994. The groundbreaking book about the dangers of DDT and the importance of various ecosystems to the health of humankind and the entire planet.

Ronald Chepesiuk, *Sixties Radicals, Then and Now: Candid Conversations with Those Who Shaped the Era*. Jefferson, NC: McFarland, 1995. This book offers interviews with men and women who led the 1960s counterculture and antiwar movements and includes stories from the past, comments on life during the 1960s, and personal visions for the future.

Phyllis Chesler, *Women and Madness*. Garden City, NY: Doubleday, 1972. An analysis of the psychology, health, and cultural roles of women during the sixties and early seventies.

Bettye Collier-Thomas and V. P. Franklin, eds., *Sisters in the Struggle*. New York: New York University Press, 2001. A collection of sixteen essays by African American women who actively participated in the civil rights and black power movements.

Vicki L. Crawford, Jacqueline Anne Rouse, and Barbara Woods, eds., *Women in the Civil Rights Movement*. Brooklyn, NY: Carlson, 1990. This book discusses black women in the civil rights movement between 1945 and 1965; it is one book in the sixteen-book series Black Women in United States History.

Sara Davidson, *Loose Change: Three Women of the Sixties*. Garden City, NY: Doubleday, 1977. The story of three young women and their exploits in college, the civil rights movement,

New Left politics, and the counterculture revolution.

Jim DeRogatis, *Kaleidoscope Eyes*. New York: Citadel, 1996. A well-informed exploration of psychedelic rock from the 1960s to the 1990s written by a senior editor of *Rolling Stone*.

Susan Dworkin, *She's Nobody's Baby: A History of American Women in the Twentieth Century*. New York: Simon & Schuster, 1983. Dworkin's work contains famous quotes and hundreds of pictures covering eight decades of major events in women's history.

Alice Echols, *Scars of Sweet Paradise*. New York: Metropolitan Books, 1999. An exploration of how blues singer Janis Joplin re-created herself as a sixties rock-and-roll superstar after leaving her small Texas town as a beatnik folksinger.

———, *Shaky Ground: The Sixties and Its Aftershocks*. New York: Columbia University Press, 2002. An analysis of the counterculture revolution and how the shake-up of social, gender, racial, musical, and cultural concepts permanently changed the world.

Lillian Faderman, *Odd Girls and Twilight Lovers*. New York: Columbia University Press, 1991. The history of lesbian life in the United States during the twentieth century.

David Farber, *The Great Age of Dreams: America in the 1960s*. New York: Hill and Wang, 1994. A history of the 1960s written from the perspective of how the Vietnam War, the rise of the counterculture, big-city riots, and other sixties conflicts disrupted the American dream.

Betty Friedan, *The Feminine Mystique*. New York: Norton, 1963. The groundbreaking book about the lives of suburban women during the early sixties and the unhappiness faced by many because of gender discrimination.

———, *It Changed My Life*. New York: Random House, 1976. This book includes excerpts of the most famous speeches and articles written by a leading women's rights activist and a founding member of the National Organization for Women.

David Lance Goines, *The Free Speech Movement: Coming of Age in the 1960s*. Berkeley, CA: Ten Speed, 1993. A book that studies the social and cultural aspects of the early 1960s Berkeley Free Speech Movement, which transformed into the antiwar movement after the United States invaded Vietnam.

Michael Gross, *My Generation*. New York: HarperCollins, 2000. This book tells the stories of numerous baby boomers, what they did during the sixties, and how they went on to become famous real-estate magnates, computer specialists, porn actresses, gay rights activists, and ultra-conservative politicians.

Gerri Hirshey, *We Gotta Get Out of This Place*. New York: Atlantic Monthly, 2001. The history of women rock-and-roll musicians in the male-dominated popular music business.

Carol Hymowitz and Michaele Weissman, *A History of Women in America*. New York: Bantam Books, 1978. A comprehensive and informative history of women in the United States from the time of the Revolutionary War to the 1970s era of feminism.

Laura Joplin, *Love, Janis*. New York: Villard Books, 1992. A biography of Janis Joplin written by her sister and based on the long, detailed letters the author had received from the singer over the years.

Kathleen Kinkade, *A Walden Two Experiment*. New York: William Morrow, 1973. Kinkade describes life during the first five years of the Twin Oaks Community, one of the era's most successful communes, founded in rural Virginia in 1967.

Blanche Linden-Ward and Carol Hurd Green, *American Women in the 1960s: Changing the Future*. New York: Twayne, 1993. A comprehensive book detailing women's roles in the culture of the 1960s in such fields as the civil

rights movement, higher education, media, and the arts.

Helena Znaniecka Lopata, *Occupation: Housewife*. New York: Oxford University Press, 1971. A sociological study of women and their roles as mothers and housewives.

Timothy Miller, *The Hippies and American Values*. Knoxville: University of Tennessee Press, 1991. A sympathetic look at the hippie lifestyle that analyzes the social conditions that spawned the counterculture.

———, *The Sixties Communes*. Syracuse, NY: Syracuse University Press, 1999. A volume that details the life and times of people practicing communal living between the early 1960s and the mid-1970s.

Joan Morrison and Robert K. Morrison, eds., *From Camelot to Kent State: The Sixties Experience in the Words of Those Who Lived It*. New York: Times Books, 1987. The personal stories of fifty-nine men and women who lived through the 1960s are presented. In their own words they recall the civil rights movement, assassinations, protesting the Vietnam War, and joining the counterculture revolution.

Leila J. Rupp and Verta Taylor, *Survival in the Doldrums*. New York: Oxford University Press, 1987. The history of the American women's rights movement in the years following World War II.

Grace Slick, *Somebody to Love?* New York: Warner Books, 1998. The self-penned story of one of rock music's most influential female vocalists as she tripped through the sixties hippie scene with Jefferson Airplane and later battled drug and alcohol addiction.

June Sochen, *Herstory.* New York: Alfred, 1974. The author, a professor of history at Northwestern University, presents the women's side of American history and details the life stories and experiences of women who helped make the United States the successful country it is today.

Amy Swerdlow, *Women Strike for Peace.* Chicago: University of Chicago Press, 1993. A historical account of Women Strike for Peace by a founding member of the organization, which brought together the peace and feminist movements during the early sixties.

David P. Szatmary, *Rockin' in Time: A Social History of Rock and Roll.* 4th ed. Prentice-Hall, 1999. An unusual study of rock genres from the 1950s to the present as they mirror the society in which they develop, including the ambitions and roles of women.

Lauri Umansky, *Motherhood Reconsidered: Feminism and the Legacies of the Sixties.* New York: New York University Press, 1996. An exploration of the women's

movement of the 1960s and its long-lasting influence on traditional women's roles in society.

Irwin Unger and Debi Unger, eds., *The Times Were a Changin'.* New York: Three Rivers, 1998. An anthology of "speeches, manifestos, court decisions, and groundbreaking journalism of the Sixties," with excerpts from documents concerning the antiwar movement, women's liberation, the race to the moon, and other compelling subjects.

John Wagner, *Sex Roles in Contemporary American Communes.* Bloomington: Indiana University Press, 1982. An analysis of religious, racial, and counterculture communes and the various roles assumed in these settings by men and women.

Bonnie Watkins and Nina Rothchild, *In the Company of Women.* St. Paul: Minnesota Historical Society, 1996. A collection of short personal stories from eighty-three women who describe the reasons they became feminists and how the women's movement has improved their lives.

Deborah Gray White, *Too Heavy a Load.* New York: Norton, 1999. This book discusses black women and their roles in the civil rights movement between 1894 and 1994.

Malcolm X, with Alex Haley, *The Autobiography of Malcolm X.* New York: Ballantine Books, 1990. The life story of one of the most famous and charismatic leaders of the black power revolution.

Periodicals

Sally Kempton, "Cutting Loose," *Esquire,* July 1970. An article about women in the radical feminist movement.

Harper Lee, "Love—in Other Words," *Vogue,* April 15, 1961. A commentary about life, love, and the human condition from the Pulitzer Prize–winning author of *To Kill a Mockingbird.* This article can be found on the web at http://mockingbird.chebucto.org/love.html.

Internet Sources

Sundiata Acoli, "A Brief History of the Black Panther Party and Its Place in the Black Liberation Movement," April 2, 1985. www.cs.oberlin.edu. An essay written by an imprisoned Black Panther member detailing the history of the Black Panther Party.

Margo Adler, "Heretic's Heart: A Journey Through Spirit and Revolution," 1997. www.straw.com. Excerpts from chapter 4 of Adler's book *Heretic's Heart: A Journey Through Spirit and Revolution,* with the author's recollections of being jailed during the FSM protests, available on a link from the Free Speech Movement Archives website.

Bettina Aptheker, "Women and the FSM," March 20, 2002. www.straw.com. Aptheker's speech about women's roles in the Free Speech Movement from the 1984 FSM reunion.

"Fannie Lou Hamer, 1917–1977," 1997. www.beejae.com. A biographical article about the civil rights leader whose experiences helped spur the passage of the 1965 Voting Rights Act.

Sonia Pressman Fuentes, "Sex Maniac," Feminism/Women in Philosophy, 1999. www.erraticimpact.com. A website with excerpts from the chapter "Sex Maniac" in Fuentes's book *Eat First—You Don't Know What They'll Give You: The Adventures of an Immigrant Family and Their Feminist Daughter.* The author was the first female lawyer hired by the EEOC during the midsixties.

Betty Gips, "Council of Spiritual Practices," CSP—Sisters of the Extreme: Women Writing on the Drug Experience, 1995–2000. http://google.yahoo.com/bin/query?p=women+on+drugs+1960s&;hc=0&;hs=0. Excerpts from the author's 1972 book *Scrapbook of a Haight Ashbury Pilgrim: Spirit, Sacraments, and Sex in 1967/1968,* taken from a review of the 2000 book *Sisters of the Extreme: Women Writing on the Drug Experience,* edited by Cynthia Palmer and Michael Horowitz and printed on the Council of Spiritual Practices website.

Melissa Hantman, "Helen Gurley Brown," Salon.com, September 26, 2000. http://dir.salon.com. An article on the Salon.com website about the author of *Sex and the Single Girl* and editor of *Cosmopolitan* magazine.

Sara Ironman, "Diane Arbus." www.temple.edu/photo/photographers/arbus/arbus.htm. The photographs, biography, and time line of the award-winning photographer's life.

John F. Kennedy, "President's Commission on the Status of Women." http://womenshistory.about.com. A website sponsored by Women's History Online with a photograph of the actual executive order creating the PCSW on December 14, 1961.

Lisa Law, "Summer of Love Photos," 1999. www.summeroflove.org. This article discusses the photos and biographical information of Lisa Law, one of the celebrated photographers of the 1960s, whose subjects included Bob Dylan, the Grateful Dead, and other rock stars.

"Linda McCartney's Sixties," Dayton Art Institute, 1998, www.daytonartinstitute.org. A profile of the celebrity photographer that accompanied a show of her work in 1998.

Pat Mainardi, "The Politics of Housework," CWLU Herstory. www.cwluherstory.com. An article posted on the Chicago Women's Liberation Union (CWLU) website that was first published in 1970 by Redstockings, an early women's liberation group centered in New York that was responsible for a number of influential writings.

Chuck Miller, "Ronnie Spector: For Every Kiss You Give Me, I'll Give You Three." http://hometown.aol.com. An article about the renowned lead singer of the Ronettes and her struggles in show business.

Eleanor Roosevelt, "My Day—Women's Issues," American Experience. www.pbs.org. A website about the PBS show *American Experience* dedicated to the former first lady and including twenty-eight of the daily syndicated columns Roosevelt wrote between 1935 and 1962 on a wide variety of issues.

Valerie Solanas, "The S.C.U.M. Manifesto." www.bcn.net/~jpiazzo/scum.htm. This website contains the thirteen-thousand-word radical feminist essay from 1967 by the Society for Cutting Up Men (S.C.U.M.), which advocates the virtual murder of all males.

UXL Biographies, "Gloria Steinem," Women's History Month website, www.galegroup.com/free_resources/. A detailed biography of the feminist leader with suggestions for further reading and links to other women's history topics.

Index

on sit-ins, 39
on women's roles, 13–14, 18–19
Fuentes, Sonia Pressman, 33–34, 36

Gardiner, Joyce, 89
Garvey, Helen, 72
gay rights, 42–44
gender discrimination, 11–12
  see also sexism; women's liberation
    movement
Ginsburg, Ruth Bader, 27
girl groups, 91–93
Goines, David Lance, 75
Grateful Dead, 76
*Great Age of Dreams; America in the
  1960s, The* (Farber), 42–43, 57
Green, Carol Hurd, 11, 64, 84, 95, 102
Greenwich, Ellie, 93

Haight-Ashbury, 76, 80
Hamer, Fannie Lou, 54–55
Harris, Duchess, 55
Hayden, Tom, 70
Height, Dorothy, 51–53
Hell's Angels, 80
Hernandez, Aileen, 55
Herstory (Sochem), 24
Hesse, Eva, 105
hippies, 76, 78
  see also communes; counterculture
    movement
History of Women in America, A
  (Hymowitz and Weissman), 22–23
Hodgkin, Dorothy C., 24
homemaking

dissatisfaction with, 18
economic basis for, 13
isolation of work of, 15
prescription drugs and, 18–19
prevalence of, 13–15
work of, 18
House Un-American Activities
  Committee, 64, 66
housewives. *See* homemaking
Human Be-In, 79–80
Hymowitz, Carol, 22–23

inner cities, 57
  see also African Americans; civil rights
    movement; riots
In the Company of Women (Watkins and
  Rothchild), 25
It Changed My Life (Friedan), 37, 41

Jackson, Mahalia, 91
Jefferson Airplane, 76, 81, 96–97
Johnson, Lyndon Baines, 61
Joplin, Janis, 97–98

Kahn, Phyllis, 34
Kempton, Sally, 42
Kennedy, John F., 28
Kesey, Ken, 76
King, Carole, 93
King, Martin Luther, Jr., 49, 51
Kinkade, Kathleen, 83, 86–87, 88

Law, Lisa, 82
Leary, Timothy, 76, 77
Leder, Kit, 85–86

Picture Credits

Cover Image: © Bettmann/CORBIS

Associated Press, AP, 38, 50, 65, 67, 73, 82, 96

© Bettmann/CORBIS, 20, 30, 31, 35, 37, 49, 52, 62, 71, 74, 81, 103

© CORBIS, 46

© Christopher Felver/CORBIS, 105

© Hulton Archive, 9, 14, 17, 25, 26, 33, 43, 57, 59, 77, 92, 94, 99, 100

National Archives, 11

Library of Congress, 54

© Ted Streshinsky/CORBIS, 68, 79, 85, 89

About the Author

Stuart A. Kallen is the author of more than 150 nonfiction books for children and young adults. He has written on topics ranging from the theory of relativity to the history of rock and roll. In addition, Mr. Kallen has written award-winning children's videos and television scripts. In his spare time, Stuart A. Kallen is a singer-songwriter-guitarist in San Diego, California.